HISTORIC HOUSES

HISTORIC HOUSES

Conversations in Stately Homes

CONDÉ NAST PUBLICATIONS LIMITED
IN ASSOCIATION WITH COLLINS - LONDON & GLASGOW

Published by CONDÉ NAST PUBLICATIONS LTD
Vogue House, Hanover Square, London, W1
in association with COLLINS – London & Glasgow

SBN 90030305 0

Condé Nast Book Department:
Editor – Alexander Kroll
Assistant Editor – Elisabeth Brayne
Art Editor – Marion Neville
Editorial – Susan Harley

Printed in England by Taylowe Ltd., Maidenhead, and bound by Hazell, Watson & Viney, Aylesbury

CONTENTS

Blenheim Palace

The photographs were taken by
Jacques Boucher – Tyninghame Castle
Anthony Denney – Mellerstain
Horst – Leixlip Castle
Dmitri Kasterine – Shugborough
Michael Wickham – Penshurst Place, Forde Abbey, Charlecote Park, Longleat House, Wilton House, The Royal Pavilion
Ray Williams – Hatfield House, Leixlip Castle, Inveraray Castle, Castle Howard, Blenheim Palace, Kedleston Hall, Weston Park, Ragley Hall, Harewood House, Shugborough, Ebberston Hall, Sezincote

A TALENT FOR SURVIVAL

As every schoolboy knows, the aristocrats of Britain were once a headstrong lot, furthering their ambitions with merciless pride.

Then came the Tudor monarchs, a tougher line than those high-born but rough-and-ready thrusters had hitherto encountered. They soon learned that if their social and material ambitions were too outrageously unbridled they must be prepared to gamble with their heads. Many of them proved that the courtier's life could offer a meteorically rewarding career, but also, too often, a short-lived one. The fates of the Duke of Northumberland, Earl of Essex, Sir Walter Raleigh and a score of other high adventurers plainly underlined that fact.

Gradually, then, post-Tudor, England's aristocracy began to settle into their domains on that more or less permanent and pacific basis which has since been their native lot, always prepared to gamble their lives in foreign wars but not their lives *and* lands in any domestic upset.

Privilege before power has been their motto. When any struggle—political, religious or social—became too sharp and rugged, they opted out. When clear-cut choices had to be made they sat athwart their farm-land fences, so to speak. In the days of religious oppression few Catholic landowners sacrificed their acres for their beliefs, preferring secret chapels and open fields. Few land-owning Royalists openly resisted Cromwell on the King's behalf. Those who did showed a venal willingness to pay their way back under the Protector, wishful once more for the security of those grazing lands and timbered slopes. They never made the same mistake again.

This practical policy has paid off handsomely in terms of peace and plenty. Even at the end of the eighteenth century, when the rest of Europe was passing through a bloody revolutionary ferment and hundreds of French aristocrats were setting themselves disdainfully under the guillotine, their English counterparts were gothicising their mansions, experimenting with new agricultural techniques, discussing new theories of the Picturesque. Above all, they were preoccupied with the impact of the Industrial Revolution—whether to ignore, accept or exploit its economic implications, for, after all, many of them had coal beneath and maturing woodlands for Britain's merchantmen and men o' war above those acres.

Thus, by shrewd management and skilful manipulation, the British aristocracy has retained its parks, farms and forests, and, even more improbably, its palaces and mansions, at a time when the nobility of other lands were hitting the dust. History records no more convincing demonstration of the profitability of passive resistance. Mahatma Gandhi might well have learned the rudiments of his philosophy by studying the Raj at home.

Even in the vast social upheavals of this century, which have seen the aristocracies of Russia, Poland, Germany, Austria and a dozen other countries decimated and those of Italy and France reduced to bit-players in *opera bouffe*, the patricians of Britain were never more securely settled

The lion in winter at Longleat

within their continuing world of privilege. In an era when Jack finally asserted—and more or less proved—that he was every whit as good as his erstwhile master, the latter may seem to have shifted his ground but somehow seems to have enlarged his grounds. We thus have today the curious paradox of an aristocracy entrenched and enriched within a social order supposedly dedicated to egalitarian principles and the diminution of those vast disparities between great wealth and extreme poverty.*

This paradox is seen in its most extreme form in the annual sums dispensed each year by British Governments (including Labour Governments) by means of the Grants to Historic Houses Committee, which, since 1953, has distributed nearly six million pounds for the improvement and maintenance of great houses. That these houses are usually in the hands of far-from-impoverished owners whose families have been around in those same houses for two centuries or more is probably little more than a curious and incidental footnote for the social historian.

Quite clearly, then, the British aristocracy has not only proved itself skilled in the arts of social adaptation and accommodation, but equally skilled in the crafts of propaganda. Their ranks include some of the most accomplished propagandists of our time, from whom advertising practitioners and PROs could learn a lot. (Indeed, the owner of one of the houses shown in this book is a successful professional PRO). Their success may well spring from the fact that they deal almost exclusively in two aspects of propaganda which are normally in short supply: truth and understatement.

They rarely lie, although they are masters of the art of telling omission. They may be short of ready money—who isn't?—and this situation they will mention with disarming carefreedom as if it were the end of an Augustian Age for themselves, only to be expected in the Age of Affluence for others. What is rarely if ever mentioned—yet it would be a reasonable and logical corollary—is the capital value of the lands, forests and farms they survey from the terraces of their colonnaded and balustraded *pianos nobiles*. Even at a modest £200 an acre few of the more substantial landowners are worth less than half-a-million pounds and many ten times that. 'But only on paper,' is the throwaway line if pressed. 'I couldn't lay my hands on any of it right now.'

Intrigued by the hearsay, rumour and legend surrounding this aspect of the aristocratic scene, but lacking first-hand expertise in the matter, I once asked Randolph Churchill to write a piece on the subject for *House & Garden* magazine. He welcomed the opportunity, for he was no obsequious respecter of place or person. He had dined in many of the great mansions he proposed to write about—even if only on the Frank Harris terms of once and never again—for he could be pugnacious, churlish, utterly impossible in the niceties of normal social exchanges.

Across the dinner-table he was frequently more than flesh-and-blood could stand, but, at his desk, with an assignment on hand, he was a demonic professional, ringing up the relevant editor—charges always reversed—to question a brief or clarify a point. His copy was invariably dead on time and he was always ready to discuss or amend a paragraph which had prompted some factual doubt or legal query. (His lay knowledge of the law, especially that of libel, was extensive and, on occasion, expensive—to others.)

In his article *Are the Stately Homes really in decline?* he made no bones about his own views in the matter. 'The modern fashion,' he wrote, 'is to bruit it around that two World Wars, penal taxation and the Welfare State, have taxed the great families of England out of existence and forced them out of their houses. In fact, it is not as bad as all that. Nearly all

Opposite *A view of the inner hall, with the entrance hall beyond, at Daylesford, Lord Rothermere's Worcestershire home, decorated by John Fowler*

*That percipient reporter, Roy Perrot, has explored this paradox at length and with sly yet sympathetic detachment in his book *The Aristocrats* (Weidenfeld & Nicolson 1968), which should be read by anyone interested in the talent for survival of the British upper crust

Two more examples of John Fowler's work at Daylesford. The Evening Room, seen opposite, has very pale grey walls, mustard-yellow upholstery and an early Victorian Needlework rug. The Drawing Room, shown above, has been restored to its original colour scheme of pale blue, grey, white and gold. The Directoire Aubusson carpet picks up all the colours in the room. In the foreground is a fine Indian carved ivory table

the proprietors of great British country houses and their children distinguished themselves in both World Wars and despite the envious Marxist propaganda which has become prevalent in the past forty or fifty years, the vast majority of the British public who live in the countryside—as opposed to those who live in urban areas—derive a positive gratification from the fact that they live in an area where their ancestors lived for many hundreds of years, and which has as its social centre a splendid house inhabited by a noble family who have usually done their duty, by the tenants, by the county and by their King and Country.'

After a quick side-swipe at the popular press, whether Socialist, Liberal or Tory, who seemed inclined always, he thought, 'to excite envy and jealousy against those who are better off than themselves,' he opined that 'the figures of those who visit the great country houses of England, which are open at two shillings or half-a-crown, indicate that the British democracy greatly prefer visiting houses that are still inhabited by the families who have lived in them for hundreds of years, than a lifeless museum, however well-stocked with the artistic treasures of the past.'

He then proceeded to list a number of owners of great houses who were living, very comfortably, in such country houses, with a sly reference to his kinsman the Duke of Marlborough who, he says, 'still manages to live on a considerable scale in the west wing of Blenheim!'*

'Of course,' Churchill went on grandiloquently, 'it goes without saying that nobody lives on the scale of 1914. The expense of domestic staff and the difficulty of procuring any form of service in some parts of the country has made everybody pull in their horns. At one of the greatest English houses there was in the 'thirties a staff of twenty-seven. Today there are nine, but the nine cost as much as the twenty-seven did before the war. Expenses have been trebled.'

The interviews and pictures in this book go a long way to substantiate Churchill's contentions. Many owners do manage to lead very agreeable lives within the straitened contemporary circumstances of their Stately Homes, although few can match the well-guarded privacy of the immensely rich Duke of Buccleuch, who lives for part of each year in each of his three magnificent but little-known houses at Boughton (Northants), Bowhill (Selkirkshire) and Drumlarrig (Thornhill). Nevertheless, they make out very comfortably.

This has been made possible by the technical skills of solicitors and accountants. Indeed, no man has been listened to more attentively in the Stately Homes during the past twenty-five years than the chartered accountant. Sometimes it is difficult to see why, for, despite Churchill's assertions, it is not all that comfortable a life that *all* owners enjoy within their great shells. Living anachronistically in one wing of a vast palace isn't necessarily all that rewarding to the soul or cosseting to the body. But roots go deep in England. Like those other islanders, the Japanese, we are great ancestor-worshippers. Merely to have had a known forebear is something to be pridefully made known to others, even though he may have been a corrupting or corrupted knave. The portrait of such a fellow or felon on the wall, plus the knowledge that he paced the same hall and terraces a century or so ago, seems curiously reassuring to the *amour propre* of an extraordinarily high number of Britons of consequence. And to Britons of lesser consequence, to judge by the alacrity with which they hasten to the College of Heralds on receiving life peerages and even more sub-standard titles, seeking out mottoes and escutcheons suitable to their new estate.

Many visitors to Britain's Stately Homes are under the impression that transferring ownership to the National Trust is a skilful device by which landowners have their cake and eat it. But this is far from the case. The National Trust has not, for several years, accepted houses without a substantial endowment, and the owners, if they still wish or are still able to live in those houses are obliged to allow the public access. Elsewhere in this book Major Sir Brian Fairfax-Lucy explains something of his feelings in having had his family home, Charlecote, handed over to the National Trust—the last, incidentally, accepted by the Trust *without* endowment. At the other end of the scale is Petworth. Lord Leconfield handed over £272,000 to the National Trust for the upkeep of that vast house. And when the 2nd Viscount Astor handed Cliveden over to the National Trust in 1942 he endowed the house with a sum of £273,000, later supplemented by his son with a covenant approaching two thousand pounds a year.

That these houses do require impressive sums for their upkeep is a recurring theme throughout these interviews. Not all British building material is of long-lasting gritstone. Some of our native building stone is tragically soft as too many Oxford Colleges now sadly demonstrate.

The Saloon at Shugborough, formerly a square dining-room until Wyatt lengthened it in 1803. The pillars were covered in plaster, but John Fowler discovered the scagliola work by Joseph Alcott underneath; the capitals were supplied by Frances Bernasconi. The room is furnished with eighteenth-century chairs, sofas and side-tables; in the foreground is a French mahogany and kingwood 'knee-hole' library table

*See pp 112/123 in this book.

So, too, with many of the Stately Homes. But grants from the Historic Houses Grants Committee have done much to preserve the fabrics, for not all owners are as resolutely determined to find the money from their own resources as is the Marquess of Salisbury (pp 41-48).

So much for the carcases of these palaces and mansions . . .

The interiors of these great houses inevitably demonstrate an extraordinary decorative diversity. Modesty and reticence were virtually unknown qualities in the men who set about building these so-called homes, whether Sir John Thynne at Longleat or Robert Cecil at Hatfield, Lord Carlisle at Castle Howard or Marlborough at Blenheim. They wished to show their individual achievement to the masses in their own time and to gain some kind of grip upon the immortality of later times. They were frequently vain, ambitious, ostentatious. They were, indeed, the equivalent of self-made tycoons of our own time. But because the chance to rise from obscurity was fairly infinitesimal and opportunities were mainly available only to a small but well-educated oligarchy, these men were also men of taste—and supremely self-confident. They knew what they wanted and went out to get it. And because they lived in an age when canons of taste were clearly established and followed, when professional arbiters of taste were also few and far between and when craftsmanship was widely practised, they were able to get for a comparative song (even by their own currency rates) those objects which now fetch such grandiose sums in the saleroom. Harewood's most notable commode cost Mr. Lascelles £86. (Today's worth? At least five hundred times that sum.) Mr. Anthony Coleridge has shown in his researches* into the relationships between Chippendale's contemporary craftsmen and clients how readily members of the eighteenth-century aristocracy, unlike their latterday descendants, responded to new fashions. The Dukes of Northumberland, Beaufort, Norfolk and Atholl were amongst the subscribers to Chippendale's *Director* issued in 1754. Could any furniture designer today interest such a ducal quartet in his published designs?

Yet there is one designer-decorator today who does exercise what is virtually a monopoly of patronage and practice in the decoration, restoration, furnishing and refurbishing of almost any great house in England or, for that matter, Scotland or Ireland. That is John Fowler. This modest scholarly man has for over a quarter-of-a-century been the authority to whom the well-born and well-heeled have turned when faced with the problems of making a Stately Home fit for twentieth-century families to live in. Amongst the houses featured in this volume, decorations at Sezincote, Shugborough, Ragley, Wilton, and Tyninghame, have been initiated and/or supervised by this unusual artist, scarcely known to the general public. His work is probably to be seen at its best in a house that is not open to the public: Lord Rothermere's house, Daylesford in Worcestershire. Two pictures from a feature on Daylesford, published a few years ago in *House & Garden*, show something of the subtle skills of Mr. Fowler in this most homely, ubiquitous yet elusive of the arts of mankind. No other designer or decorator of our time has imaginative authority comparable with that of Mr Fowler, who has managed the vastly tricky job of decorating eighteenth-century houses in a manner that is authentic yet never pompous and—the rarest gift of all—is never pastiche.

In the main the houses shown in this book are vast. They would be daunting enterprises for anybody to own and run. No matter how much underpinning we were promised, most of us would run a mile from the responsibility of owning such splendiferous assemblies of stone, bricks

Rolls-Royce Rally 1969, in the grounds of Blenheim Palace

**Chippendale Furniture* The Work of Thomas Chippendale and his Contemporaries in the Rococo Taste: Vile, Cobb, Langlois, Channon, Hallett, Ince and Mayhew, Lock, Johnson and others circa 1745-1765. (Faber & Faber 1968)

and mortar, furniture and flora. Spare a thought, then, for the National Trust which owns or holds in trust approximately 120 of what might be termed great country houses and over 1,000 of somewhat lesser houses. Plus as many gardens. Few institutions in the history of this country have bestowed so much innocent pleasure upon so many people at so little cost as the National Trust.

Only two of the houses shown in this book are in the care of the National Trust: Shugborough and Charlecote. The others remain in private ownership, although the public is admitted at specified times (except to Sezincote, which remains essentially a private house). The houses have been chosen to span almost the full range of English domestic architecture of the more impressive order, from Penshurst to the Royal Pavilion. Wilton, which has frequently been called the most beautiful house in England, is here. So, too, is what is certainly the largest house in England—Blenheim—justifiably known as a Palace. But not all beautiful houses are great houses. There is one house in this book which is small, judged by the most searching standards of suburbia. Ebberston Hall, in Yorkshire, could be, for many Britons, the most beautiful house in the land. A pity that our eighteenth-century nabobs were quite so ostentatious. A few more Ebberstons dotted around this still-pleasant land would have been one of the most pleasing legacies that century of taste could have left us. But they did us proud all the same. As did the aristocrats and their architects and decorators of the fifteenth, sixteenth, and seventeenth centuries. Are we doing as well by the twenty-first and twenty-second centuries? For the architectural enthusiast particularly interested in the incomparably rich domestic buildings of these islands and not yet brainwashed by the jargon of planners' language and the incomprehensibility of planning dreams for New Towns, nuclear plants, power stations, airports, motorways, development areas, environmental areas, overspill areas, the answer may well be a dyspeptic negative.

Part of the pleasure in compiling a series of interviews of this kind derives from comparing the similarities and disparities of the owners, and in seeking to discover whether life in these vast houses imposes any kind of recognizable pattern upon them.

Certain characteristics do keep cropping up. Most of the owners are no longer young but almost all look younger than their years, sometimes by a decade or more. This youthful longevity doubtless springs from the vigorously outdoor lives that most of them choose to lead. Then again, most of them live simply and thriftily, in sharp contrast to some of their early predecessors who frequently started to build their great houses with a flourish and then couldn't afford to finish—as at Ragley and Mellerstain. And few owners nowadays entertain on any grand scale; content, it seems, to eat for 365 days a year in small dining-rooms in remote wings, leaving the State Dining Room, complete with appropriately glittering plate, for inspection by the masses. The only scion in these notes with anything like the extroverted panache and bravura of his forebears is probably Lord Lichfield, who has energy and flair enough for a Regency blade. He sometimes has a score of week-end guests. But he, after all, is the youngest of the personalities interviewed here.

Another common thread is recollections of the fearsome chills of these mansions, Geoffrey Roper, now in his seventies, recalls early shivering days in Forde Abbey: 'The temperature in the house could literally take one's breath away'; Lord Lichfield, barely thirty, recalls his infancy at Shugborough: 'The ink froze in the ink-well in my room'. Now central heating has come to the Stately Homes as well as to suburbia, but will future patricians cossetted by oil-fired, gas-fired heating devices live as long as these men with their frozen memories?

Land, of course, is, without any exception, their collective passion. To sell an acre is, for them, a tragedy verging on suicide or, at least, genocide. If forced to sell anything the jewellery goes first (tough on milady, perhaps, but better times will come and tiaras can be hired); followed by the gold and silver plate, then the furniture, then the pictures in a rough order of what might be termed The Incidence of Replaceability. Land, now virtually irreplaceable, can only be wrung out of them outside the very doors of Bankruptcy Court, for they long ago learned that upon ownership of those loams, gravels and greensands their wealth and privilege are ultimately based. But the land isn't, for them, merely another kind of long-term banking device. It is an essential feature in their quest for survival. They work their lands today as skilfully and experimentally as ever Coke of Holkham Hall did his farms in Norfolk. Under energetic direction, the agricultural output from Harewood's 7,000 acres, sliced by death duties to a third of what it was thirty years ago, is now far greater than from the original acreage. Owners are now working farmers, personally involved and deeply committed in these enterprises, keeping a watchful eye on their tenants and choosing the Home Farm agent with at least the same care that they would give to the choice of a son or daughter-in-law—and with probably rather more say in the matter.

Their woodlands, particularly, are very much a personal matter, not only as cover for the rearing of their little targets for the shooting season but also as a crop. They know their trees as well as their shepherds know their flocks. They may no longer grow oaks with the certainty of knowledge of their forefathers, knowing that England would always need those wooden men o'war, but they know their markets pretty well. When the bottom drops out of the pit-prop market they move into other realms, growing for more mundane needs, planting quick-growing species that will have a market well within half-a-century. To this end they are out and about in their woodlands for long hours, planting as though they will live for a century to see the results.

Finally, that point about seeing crowds of people wandering round their pleasances—do they really mind?

Curiously enough, they seem not unduly perturbed. For one thing, this pastime of country-house visiting has long been a characteristic of the English countryside. Heaven knows why, when we are, especially our upper crust, such a passionately private, introverted, inhibited lot. But there it is. Perhaps the owners of these Stately Homes have, as usual, been brainwashed by their own traditions. Whatever the reason, they all seem only too willing to see other people wandering about, through their parterres, over their sward and up into their woods. And it's not just the half-crowns, useful though they are. Perhaps Geoffrey Roper sums up part of the general feeling when he says 'If one has the good fortune to own and live in a beautiful place, then, in a sense, its beauties and history ought to be shared, especially the gardens.' Perhaps the Marquess of Bath sums up the other part with his laconic comment that: 'I don't get to know 'em, so I can't say I like 'em or dislike 'em. The main thing is I need visitors. Longleat needs eight thousand a year for the next ten years to cope with woodworm alone . . .'

Such are a few of the pleasures and problems of owning a Stately Home in the 1970s.

ROBERT HARLING
Editor House & Garden

The hall in Lord Lichfield's private apartments at Shugborough decorated by David Mlinaric. An example of Mlinaric's striking use of colour throughout can be seen in the way the warm peach stippled walls blend with the original pale stone floor

PENSHURST PLACE

ANY APPROACH to Penshurst gives the visitor a sense of delighted astonishment that so beautiful a building could stand so well preserved after six centuries of sometimes violent history—not least in our own time.

There are two main approaches to the house, both oblique. One is by way of a broad drive between herbaceous borders whereby the house, with its venerable walls and crenelated silhouette, is glimpsed between walls and high yew hedges. An alternative approach is by a sharp left turn at the gates, thence by a flight of stone steps, succeeded by a path between hedges. Whereupon the full magnificence of the south front is viewed.

Both approaches lead to the terrace upon which the house stands, overlooking the Italian garden.

The foundations of a pre-Conquest house are known to exist beneath the north front of Penshurst Place. Yet it is the house built in 1340 by Sir John de Pulteney that is the heart of Penshurst and with which the visitor today will be most absorbingly concerned. The Baron's Hall, built in 1341, is the finest domestic hall of the fourteenth century now remaining in this country. With its magnificent windows and their beautiful Kentish tracery; the Minstrels' Gallery beneath a spacious open-timbered roof, supported on beams in turn seemingly supported on ten grotesque figures or corbels (modelled on men and women who worked on Pulteney's lands) and with the original fireplace with andirons for the support of great blazing logs, this room evokes more clearly than any scholarly monograph the atmosphere of the early Great Halls of medieval England.

Of the same period is the Solar or Withdrawing-Room reached by a stone staircase from the Hall. In the Middle Ages the ladies of the household withdrew here to peer at proceedings in the Hall below through a slit window in one wall. This room is now the State Dining-Room, still used on special occasions.

The first extension of the Pulteney house was made by Henry V's brother, the Duke of Bedford. This is wrongfully yet lastingly known as the Buckingham Building, thanks to the association of Penshurst with three Dukes of Buckingham who owned Penshurst from 1447 until 1521. These additions, made in the mid-fifteenth century, include Queen Elizabeth's Room and the Tapestry Room (so-called because of three Brussels tapestries hanging there), apartments of somewhat rare grandeur for that time.

The most remarkable of later buildings is the Long Gallery (still with its original panelling), four steps up from the Buckingham group of buildings, which was begun by Sir Philip Sidney's younger brother Robert, who also built the Nether Gallery, by means of which the house is connected with the gardens, with their yewed hedge walks and terraces.

Opposite *The South Front of Penshurst Place, overlooking the Italian Garden*

Lord De L'Isle with a bust of William IV
Opposite *The private drawing-room was gothicized early in the nineteenth century by John Biagio Rebecca. More recent redecoration has emphasized the light-hearted gothick aspects of the room. The turreted Siena marble chimneypiece was designed by Rebecca*

ALTHOUGH built long before Queen Elizabeth came to the throne, Penshurst evokes the Elizabethan age as does no other house in England, not even Wilton.

Pacing the lawns or the Long Gallery, few visitors would be unduly alarmed or even surprised to come upon a chattering far-from-ghostly group in doublets and finery awaiting a call to dine.

There is no particular reason why this Elizabethan aura should cling so nostalgically and emphatically to Penshurst. Rather the reverse. But it does.

A London wool merchant built the house, with its Baron's Hall, the finest fourteenth-century domestic hall remaining in this country, in about 1340. A century later Henry V's brother, the Duke of Bedford, was enlarging the house. Then followed three Dukes of Buckingham, the third of whom fell foul of Henry VIII, lost his head to the axe and his house to the king.

Five years after succeeding to the throne Edward VI bestowed the house on Sir William Sidney, a gift appropriately if quaintly acknowledged in a stone panel inset above the great doors of the Penshurst gatehouse:

> The Most Religious and Renowned Prince Edward the Sixth, Kinge of England, France, and Ireland, gave this House of Pencester with the Mannors, Landes, and Appurtenances thereunto belonginge unto his trustye and well-beloved Servant, Syr William Sydney, Knight Banneret, serving him from the tyme of his Birth unto his Coronation in the Offices of Chamberlain and Steward of his Household; in Commemoration of which most worthy and famous Kinge, Sir Henry Sydney Knight of the Most Noble Order of the Garter, Lord President of the Council, Established in the Marches of Wales, Sonne and Heyre to the aforenamed Sir William caused this Tower to be buylded, and that most Excellent Princes Armes to be erected—Anno Domini 1585.

Thus began the Sidney's long holding of Penshurst Place.

They saw little enough of their manor in the early years. Sir William's son, Sir Henry—sponsor of the stone panel mentioned above—served Elizabeth as Lord Deputy of Ireland as well as Lord President of the Marches of Wales, but still found time to build the north and south fronts of the house.

Then came the first legend of Penshurst, for Sir Henry's son was Sir Philip, poet, diplomat, courtier and soldier, who, dying youthfully and chivalrously fighting the Spaniards in Holland, brought immortality to his name.

Philip's younger brother, Robert, added the two galleries to the house whilst continuing the family tradition of oversea service for the Crown, which has continued down to the present day. The present owner, Lord De L'Isle, was Governor General of Australia from 1961 until 1965.

Penshurst and its gardens make a rare and handsome unity. Each seems part of the other, each a perfect complement (and compliment) to the other.

Hence, perhaps, the extraordinary serenity of this castellated stone house set within ancient brick walls, yew hedges and formal gardens, and overlooking, from its modest escarpment, the gentle wooded hills above the Medway Valley.

The move from the gardens into the high and echoing Baron's Hall is a translation into another world. The Hall, built more than six hundred years ago, is surprisingly well preserved, especially in view of the depredations suffered by Penshurst during the eighteenth century when it was on the verge of becoming yet another romantic ruin.

The timbered roof (of chestnut, not oak) rises over sixty feet above a Minstrels' Gallery, central hearth and warming, red-brick floor. On the hearth a double trestle of wrought iron recalls its long-ago function as a support for burning logs. Few buildings in Britain provide so clear a picture of the world of the Middle Ages as this house within a house.

The splendidly vaulted Crypt, which leads out of the Hall, now houses a carefully maintained collection of European medieval and renaissance armour, ranging from pikes to William IV's naval sword, from early firearms to a steel helmet—a morion—weighing nearly twenty pounds, a somewhat daunting headpiece for even the most hazardous of martial operations.

Other rooms open to the public include the State Dining-Room, Queen Elizabeth's Room, the Tapestry Room, the Page's Room and the Long Gallery. This magnificent chamber was begun in 1599 by Sir Philip Sidney's younger brother, Robert, and is over eighty feet long, lit by windows on three sides and thus open to all available sunlight. The room still has its original panelling with exquisitely carved wafer-thin pilasters of a rare and delicate elegance. Thence into the Nether Gallery before returning once more to the gardens.

The present owner of this legendary house is William Sidney, Lord De L'Isle, VC, now in his late fifties, tall, grey-haired, vigorous, young-looking.

He moves around his house with the relaxed assurance of a man well-acquainted with its history and legends—biographical and architectural—and ready to answer any questions likely to be fired at him. He is one of the few Stately Home owners who can reach out—and find—in his book-shelves Professor Colvin's *Biographical Dictionary of English Architects* and know his way around the scholarly entries. A visitor, admiring the chimneypiece of Siena marble in the private drawing-room, is shown the reference to J(ohn?) B(iagio?) Rebecca in Colvin and told that a note signed with the full authentic signature, John Biagio Rebecca, was discovered recently in a secret cupboard. He was the architect responsible for the Regency gothick alterations made to Penshurst in 1819—with highly successful decorative results.

As becomes a soldier, Lord De L'Isle also knows his way amongst the armour in the Baron's Hall and in the Crypt. And as a chartered accountant and business man he knows the hard basic facts and £ s d of keeping a great house from decay in the twentieth century. To this end he was prepared, two years ago, to combine nerve and expertise to chance his arm and raise the admission price to Penshurst. His resolution paid off: more and more visitors flock here where all sideshows are eschewed and where they are offered simply the enjoyment of a perambulation through one of the most interesting houses in Europe, in an unspoilt setting of walled gardens and ancient park.

The private rooms of Penshurst virtually adjoin the State rooms now open to the public. The house is thus free, to an unusual degree, from that depressing sense of separation and desolation which afflicts so many great houses in which the family lives in a corner of a remote wing. The gothick drawing-room, recently redecorated, has a yellow Coles wallpaper, printed from old blocks, yellow silk curtains and a magnificent pair of painted commodes, probably French, flanking the Rebecca chimneypiece. The dining-room opens out of this room. Across the vestibule is another more casual sitting-room.

The visitor cannot help but observe that Penshurst seems unusually lived-in, as it were, for a Stately Home. Does the owner spend much time here?

The Long Gallery which, with a similar gallery below, was begun by Sir Philip Sidney's younger brother Robert in 1599. The panelling is still the original, although the Jacobean-style plaster ceiling was installed earlier in this century. This gallery, used for exercise in poor weather, is lit on three sides and thus open to sunlight throughout the day
Opposite *A corridor in the private apartments*

'Yes, of course. We have a small flat in London, but I try to spend as much as possible of my life here.'

'Your own rooms seem very comfortable, especially after the Baron's Hall.'

'We've managed to do quite a lot of modernization in our domestic arrangements.'

'The house seems to have been built of a kind of sandstone. Is that local?'

'Yes, all the stone comes from local quarries.'

'Tougher than most sandstones, one hopes.'

'Yes, it keeps a good hard surface, and we have no industrial smoke to contend with. I'm now experimenting with a chemical formula for strengthening the surface of the stone of some of the window mullions where they've decayed. I have to thank my lucky stars that my grandfather almost broke himself restoring the fabric during the last century. He reroofed the whole place. Only a multi-millionaire could do that today.'

'When did you inherit Penshurst?'

'In 'forty-five. Just after the war.'

'From your father?'

'No, an uncle. He was a bachelor who lived until he was ninety-one. He was actually born during the Crimean War. He loved the place and looked after it devotedly. But as a bachelor he wasn't so interested in the interior.'

'Was it in good order when you inherited?'

'Basically. But we'd had three flying bombs fall within a quarter of a mile. Every window in the place was either cracked, smashed or non-existent. It was no picnic. Happily, the place was well-built by those Kentish craftsmen.'

'How long did it take you to get the place straight?'

'Well, we opened a year later. We worked pretty hard. My first wife was absolutely marvellous in the way she tackled this rather overwhelming problem.'

'Did you open to paying customers?'

'Of course. The house was first open seventy years ago at a shilling a head. It's a moot point, but we must have been the first, or almost the first, Stately Home to charge. My grandfather was certainly before his time. And we had visitors coming here for ages before that. The first visitors' book is dated eighteen hundred and eighteen.'

'Did you know you'd inherit?'

'Yes. My father was the youngest of four brothers, three of whom inherited. He only survived his brother a few months, alas. None of his brothers had any children. It was clear that if I got through the war it would be mine one day.'

'Did you know it well?'

'I spent most of the school holidays here. Luckily, my uncle liked me.'

'Did you in any way make any particular personal plans and preparations against the day you'd be responsible for Penshurst?'

'In a kind of way, I suppose I did. It was quite clear that I'd need to make my own way in the world. So after Cambridge—and I came down in the middle of the 'thirty-one slump—I trained as an accountant, paying for the privilege to serve my articles. I'm sure it was worth while.'

'What did you read at Cambridge?'

'Classics and history.'

'You seem steeped in the history of this house.'

'I don't call myself a scholar in architecture or history, but I do know this house and its contents. I wrote and published the guide which we sell here. I naturally know better than anyone else what I want to express.'

'Has your business training helped?'

'Yes it has. The object is to run the place at a profit. So far we've not asked for any government grants. I like my independence.'

'You seem to keep very much in touch with the world at large through your business life?'

'Yes. I'm chairman of Phoenix Assurance. Before I went to Australia I was an Executive Director of Schweppes. I enjoy the contrast between life here and in London. I should hate the monotony of a life of routine.'

'What about the years before you came here?'

'I had six years in the Army. I was a Grenadier.'

'Did you enjoy soldiering?'

'Yes, it teaches one a great deal. And I'm glad to say my son's a soldier. He likes it, too.'

'How do you manage to keep so large a garden going?'

'The answer is management and mechanization. We concentrate on the hedges, the roses and the borders. It's what visitors seem to like most.'

'How many visitors do you get?'

'Last year we passed the fifty thousand mark.'

'The reason?'

'A lot of people seem to want a day's peace in the country.'

Two views of the Baron's Hall, the finest surviving domestic hall of the fourteenth century, showing examples of the Penshurst armour

Opposite *The Solar or State Dining Room, the Withdrawing-Room of the original house built by Sir John Pulteney in 1340*
Above *The lower garden at Penshurst*
Below *The doorway to the King's Tower on the north front*

'How long are you open for?'

'From Easter until September, but most visitors come between May and August, and we concentrate our efforts on these months.'

'Do you have guided parties?'

'We used to, but nowadays most people prefer to be left to find their own way round. So I've had a lot of guide-cards printed—enlarged from electric typewriter type, by the way—and visitors can learn as they go, so to speak. And there are ladies with all the answers sitting in the State Rooms.'

'Do you mind having people in and around your house all through the summer months?'

'No, not a bit. We've got some privacy if we need it. Economic reasons apart, it's part of the English country house tradition that visitors are welcome.'

'Do you farm yourself?'

'Yes, and we're now in the middle of planning a new set of farm buildings. There has been an agricultural revolution and we're doing our best to meet it. It's more difficult to adapt old farm buildings to modern farming practice than an old house like this to modern living conditions!'

'How could you bear to uproot yourself to go to Australia?'

'A week to make up our minds. So we went. It's happened before. It's usually best to jump in the deep end.'

'Did you like Australia?'

'Enormously. We hope to go back this year. But wherever one is, one's home is never far from one's mind.'

Little wonder, for Penshurst is still the house that Sir Philip Sidney undoubtedly had in mind when he wrote in *The Arcadia:* 'Built of fair and strong stone, not affecting so much any extraordinary kind of fineness, as an honourable representing of a firm stateliness.'

Words, strangely enough, despite the ravages of Time and Man, still applicable to Penshurst today.

FORDE ABBEY

IN COMMON with many other renowned English country houses the origins of Forde Abbey were monastic. The Abbey was dissolved in 1539, but several of the earlier buildings remain, including the Chapter House (12th century), the cloister range (13th century) and later sixteenth-century buildings sponsored by the last abbot, Thomas Chard.

The buildings passed though various hands during the next hundred years before being bought in 1649 by Edmund Prideaux, a Devon lawyer and M.P. for Lyme Regis and later Solicitor-General.

Prideaux was undoubtedly a man of unusual architectural taste, discernment and knowledge, for by skilful rebuilding and the imaginative introduction of later structural elements he imposed upon the miscellaneous buildings he had acquired a distinct neo-classical symmetry. As a Man of Taste of his time he sought to follow certain of Palladio's tenets in establishing a major central block, connected by intervening subsidiary ranges of pavilions. In his plans he showed his discernment by adding a central block (to accommodate his major innovation, the Grand Staircase) to the existing gate tower, but allowed the tower to retain its major significance in the elevation. The composition is a masterly essay in establishing an apparently symmetrical architectural composition upon a far-from-symmetrical group of buildings, an unusual accomplishment, especially for a mid-seventeenth century architect.

There are, perhaps inevitably, legends that Inigo Jones had a hand in the design of the house that superseded the monastic buildings, but the legend seems to have little or no substance. As with other seventeenth-century houses, Prideaux may well have been his own architect, seeking technical advice from an eminent mason. In this connexion the name of Peter Mills (1600-1670), a Surveyor appointed by the City after the Great Fire, has been suggested.

The interior of the house still largely follows the general disposition of apartments that Prideaux introduced and retains much of the magnificent woodwork that he commissioned, notably in the Great Hall. Throughout the house the carving pays witness to Prideaux's standing as a patron of unusually advanced taste, with a real if tentative feeling for the new classicism, which is also shown in the chimneypieces. The plasterwork of the ceilings is generally of a less sophisticated order, possibly by the Abbotts, a Barnstaple family of plasterers, of some considerable local renown, working perhaps under the remote direction of designs supplied from a London source.

After Prideaux's death the house passed to his son, thence to a series of direct and indirect descendants until 1846. In 1864 the house was acquired by Mrs Bertram Evans of whom the present owner, Geoffrey Roper is a descendant. Few other houses have remained so comparatively unaltered over so long a period; Forde remains one of the most interesting and beautiful houses evolved mainly during the Commonwealth era.

Opposite *Looking across one of the ornamental ponds to the South Front of the Abbey*

Geoffrey Roper in his portico flower stall
Opposite *The Saloon, enlarged in the mid-seventeenth century, has a coved ceiling and doors opening on to a balcony with magnificent views of the Park*

As with so many of Britain's magnificent country houses, Forde Abbey needs some seeking out. Three miles south of the A30 route from Salisbury to the West, sheltered by a network of narrow lanes and folds of the Dorset-Somerset border hills, the great warm-toned house is set snugly within its sizable domain—and seems content to stay that way for another eight hundred years or so.

The history and architecture of the great house are dominated by one of the most ruthless actions of a ruthless king: the dissolution of the monasteries, an operation which continued from 1536-39, and which extinguished over 600 monasteries, most of which are now no more than heaps of stones. Less than two hundred remain, converted to parish churches, houses or farm buildings.

Before that dissolution, Forde had been a monastic foundation: afterwards the Abbey sank gradually into decay, its buildings unwanted, the beautiful stonework pillaged for other structures. Not until the seventeenth century was the Abbey rescued to become once more a living house, but this time a home for an ambitious magnifico.

From the twelfth century onwards, the Cistercians, a branch of the Benedictine order, had made Forde into one of the major religious foundations of England. Indeed, according to Thomas Fuller, the reliable seventeenth-century historian, the Abbey under its early thirteenth-century abbot, John, 'had more learning therein than three convents of the same bignesse anywhere in England.'

The last of the thirty-two abbots of Forde was Thomas Chard, who succeeded in 1521. He was plainly one of those men of resolution, energy, learning and imagination that the monastic orders so frequently threw up, even in the years of their decline. Thomas devoted such considerable care to the Abbey buildings that in 1539 (when Henry VIII ordered the dissolution of the larger monasteries) Forde was, according to contemporary records, in superlative and thriving order.

After the eviction of the monks, the Abbey suffered from a series of uncaring secular owners interested only in the agricultural possibilities of the estate. Sir Edmund Prideaux, Cromwell's attorney-general, was Forde's rescuer. In his rescue operations he undoubtedly destroyed a good deal of the earlier structure, but he can be forgiven those depredations, for he also gave the house that domestic grandeur which attends Forde today.

Forde is thus a medley of architectural styles. Of the earliest work little but the Chapter-House remains, although the thirteenth-century Dormitory, Undercroft and Refectory remain, lastingly evocative of the monastic provenance of the house.

Then comes the sixteenth-century work sponsored by Thomas Chard, comprising the Great Hall and Cloisters. Despite the demolition of much of Chard's work in the succeeding centuries these buildings, which still stand, do give the house its architectural character, imposing their monastic manner upon the seventeenth-century alterations and additions made by Sir Edmund, which transformed Forde from an abbey into the notable English country house which the visitor sees today.

The great façade faces a gently rising landscape of lawns and magnificent trees. Away to the right is the long walk, the borders planned in sections of contrasting colours—blue, yellow, red, yellow, blue—at their best in July, August and September.

The visitor to Forde Abbey is apt to be met in the drive by the owner, Geoffrey Roper, for he is scarcely ever out of the garden. Armed with shears, secateurs or hoe he is invariably in a strategic position to note new arrivals and to supervise the needs of his considerable acreage.

'I put in an average of twelve hours a day,' he says, 'and as I get older I seem to spend longer and longer hours out here. That's one of the curious things about old age. One expects a quieter life, diminishing responsibilities and so on. Instead, more and more things pile up. So many things still remain to be done. It's never-ending.'

'The garden has been a major interest throughout your life?'

'That and the house, of course. After all, I've spent the greater part of my life here and much of that time has been spent in making the garden, taking on from where my father left off. Now, I suppose, it's reckoned by the experts to be a very fine garden, and that inevitably means more and more of one's time to keep it that way. Not that I mind the job, but one would like to be forty years younger and starting from where one is now.'

These laments for lost years come oddly from a man who looks well over a decade younger than his years. He is of middle height, with a ruddy outdoor complexion, shy gentle manner, but of a no-nonsense directness in conversation. In his blue shirt and cord slacks, with shears in one hand and steel in the other he looks—and is—ready for full-blooded arboreal and/or horticultural action.

'What kind of garden did you take over?'

'Well, its outlines were fairly well-established by the Gwyns who owned Forde during the eighteenth century. During their ownership the lawns and drives were laid out, the ponds dug and so on. But as far as one can judge from records and legends, several of their planned innovations weren't carried out, though some of the larger trees certainly date from that time.'

'What happened during the Victorian era?'

'Herbert Evans owned the place then and he also planted some of the fine trees we have here, but to my mind he also overloaded the garden with too many shrubberies, laurels and the rest. Nevertheless, I've had reason to be thankful for much of his work, although whether it is easier to thin out than plant afresh is a moot point.'

'How many gardeners help you now?'

'Three. Fortunately my eldest son, who's still only in his very early thirties, has taken over a sizable part of the place. He always wanted to come here and after Cambridge he moved right in. He sometimes seems to me to have the energy of five men. He's put in hand schemes that take my breath away. Black-currants on a commercial scale, for instance. Over forty tons last year. Instead of coasting along with the garden we've now got a great new infusion of activity.'

'You don't seem unduly upset.'

'Indeed, no. One thanks God for one's good fortune. None of my other children showed the same gardening inclinations. They knew what they wanted to do from the word go and I encouraged them, whilst blessing my luck. A rare thing these days, I sometimes think. So many young people seem unable to make up their minds what they want to do. I've one son in Reuters, another, a doctor, in the Far East, and my daughter is a nurse at St Thomas's.

'And you spend all your time here?'

'Apart from schooldays and so on I've been here for over sixty years. My parents came here when I was five—in nineteen hundred and six—and I've been here ever since.'

'When did you decide that Forde Abbey was going to be a life's work, so to speak?'

The Great Hall was built in the sixteenth century and the panelling was added in the eighteenth century. The refectory table was constructed in the hall in 1947 from an oak grown on the estate
Opposite *One of the private rooms with tapestries and ornate ceiling*

'Long before I took over on my own account, some forty years ago.'

'And you've never regretted the decision?'

'Indeed, no. Forde is such a marvellous place. I've loved every minute of my life here. But, of course, keeping up a place like this in these days is a full-time job. As I tell my friends, we shall be the last unpaid resident caretakers. I'm now getting on for seventy. My son and daughter-in-law—she's twenty one—are far too comfortably placed in the estate cottage we converted and enlarged for them. They'd take a lot of winkling out of that, and I can't blame 'em. A few winters back we had four tons of snow come through the dormitory roof. That took some shifting—and it had to be done post-haste. That gives you an idea of the sudden blows that can hit an ancient structure like this. Since then it has been rebattened with felt underneath so it can never happen again.'

'Living in Forde Abbey has its austere moments, then?'

'Well, we're better off than we were, of course. We've now got central heating in the wing we live in, but the rest of the house doesn't have it, and I can't think it ever will. The cost would be prohibitive. I can still remember—as a child—going into the house in the winter when the temperature could literally take one's breath away. It was far warmer outside than inside on almost any winter's day.'

'The monks took it in their stride as a penitential pastime no doubt?'

'They may have done, but they also took jolly good care to dress for the conditions. They wore those very warm habits during the day, working, studying, praying—but they also slept in them, too. Not like ourselves getting out of warm clothes and into cold pyjamas. They were very practical men.'

Mrs Roper moves towards the house—from the garden, needless to say. She has been picking flowers for an annual visit from the local Women's Institute. They are coming that evening and it's plainly an important event in their calendar. The Ropers seem to be getting ready in a big way. Conversation about the house is resumed after some discussion about the flowers.

'Maintenance of the Abbey must, presumably, take a good deal of cash?'

'It's a constant dipping into funds, despite the fact that we try to limit the outgoings to the barest essential work, repairing roofs, repointing walls, looking after the fabric generally and being extremely watchful for woodworm.'

'The contents are priceless, too, one imagines.'

'The tapestries are irreplaceable. How can one replace a tapestry that took a renaissance craftsman a year to weave one square yard?'

'Do you get help from the Government?'

'The Grants to Historic Houses people are marvellous. Wholly sympathetic and understanding. But, of course, they want to see a return for their investments, and that means that in accepting a grant for the repair of a roof—look at that expanse—they ask for more visitors to be allowed into the Abbey. Fair enough. In the early days we had six open days a season perhaps. Now we have three a fortnight, apart from the visits from local groups such as the Women's Institute and so on, who come at the invitation of my wife.'

'Do you mind the crowds?'

'Not really; not at all, in fact. If one has the good fortune to own and live in such a beautiful and historic place, then, in a sense, its beauties and history ought to be shared, especially the gardens. And, generally speaking, people are quite civilized. We have no great piles of litter and so on.'

'There's great variety here—in the planting and visual pleasures. The Beech House is particularly enchanting. How much was your handiwork?'

Opposite, above *The vaulted Monks' Dormitory is 160 feet long and has original thirteenth-century single-light windows; the gun is an eighteenth-century French pinnace gun*

Below *The Cloisters, with Purbeck marble pillars contrasting with ornate sixteenth-century Perpendicular work, were reconstructed by Thomas Chard*

Right *Four different aspects of Forde Abbey showing a medley of architectural styles*

'I'm glad you like the Beech House. I began to make it some thirty-five years ago. I thought it would be a good idea to have a shelter by the Big Pond made wholly of beech and there it is, walled and roofed in beech. I roofed it in five years. Not bad going.'

'What is your particular pride in the garden?'

'Well, our giant lilies towards the first week in July are pretty memorable. They're ten to twelve feet high. I grew them from seed. They took eight years to mature. But it was well worth the effort, I think. And the collection and cultivation of the magnolias, rhododendrons and azaleas here have given me, and I hope others, enormous pleasure.'

'The garden seems to have been a continuous series of projects over the past half-century. Have you any sizable current plans?'

'I'm just beginning a project that some people might think mad for a man of my years. I've a considerable project for an arboretum in the park. Perhaps that sounds over-ambitious, even a presumptuous programme, but I feel that one must do these things. Our forebears did and we must do the same, especially in an age when there are so many influences at work destroying these things. I've calculated—or one of my sons did—that I've probably planted the best part of half-a-million trees. To my mind, that's one of the most rewarding things one can do for posterity.'

'Do you farm?'

'Not myself. We have about seventeen hundred acres here. Five farms are in the hands of tenants, and my son has a nursery of twenty-two acres of black-currants.'

He moves towards the house, going in by the door of the late Perpendicular-Gothic tower into the Great Hall built by Thomas Chard.

The Grand Staircase has richly-carved banisters with the same design painted on the wall panels
Opposite *The Oak Room, built by Prideaux, is above the Cloisters and has a fine seventeenth-century plaster ceiling*

Few owners of great houses are so well acquainted with the history of their bricks and mortar as Geoffrey Roper. He knows, and plainly loves, every stone of the place and is as knowledgeable about the painting of the ceilings as about the provenance of the remarkable Mortlake tapestries that decorate the walls of the Saloon. These tapestries, as rare and unique as any in England, were woven by the craftsmen from Brussels brought over by Charles I to work at Mortlake and are based on the Raphael cartoons now in the Victoria & Albert Museum, although the borders may well derive from original designs by Rubens. The tapestries were presented by Queen Anne to her Secretary at War, Sir Francis Gwyn, then owner of Forde, in recognition of his contribution to the war in the Netherlands. There is another version of the story which suggests that as the tapestries fit the dimensions of the walls so exactly, they may have been promised by Cromwell to Prideaux who built the room to house them. But no documentation exists to substantiate history or legend.

History and legend abound at every turn at Forde Abbey. The vicissitudes of the tapestries are matched, for instance, by the history of the two storeys of the Refectory, a wing of the thirteenth-century building, which was thus divided in the fifteenth century after the Cistercian insistence upon a vegetarian regimen was removed. An upper refectory was thereupon incorporated within the Refectory to house the carnivorous members of the community.

Even a bed in the Oak Room has its appropriate anecdote: that it was prepared for a visit by Queen Anne to her Secretary at War. But she, alas, never did make the visit.

Such stories are features inseparable from so historic a house, with its Purbeck marble-pillared cloisters; its magnificent Undercroft (where visitors take tea); its high and noble rooms; above all, its wide and beautiful gardens with their poignantly beautiful walks and timbered slopes.

HATFIELD HOUSE

HATFIELD HOUSE in Hertfordshire is built on the site of what was once known as 'Bishops Hatfield', a red brick building with Great Hall, Solar Room, and various withdrawing rooms, bedrooms, butteries and kitchens set around an inner courtyard, built at the end of the fifteenth century by Cardinal Morton, Bishop of Ely, who stood high in the favour of Henry VII. The Great Hall, as it is now known, has a magnificent oak and chestnut roof and now serves as a restaurant.

Part of this palace is incorporated in the present Hatfield House built by Robert Cecil, first Earl of Salisbury, after King James I had expressed the wish to acquire the Cecils' own house, Theobalds, on the other side of Hertfordshire, offering Hatfield in exchange. Salisbury prudently accepted the King's *quid pro quo*, whether willingly or not we do not know. With that passion for building and rebuilding, which seems to have run like a fever through the Elizabethan gentry and aristocracy, he certainly set about tearing down the old house, utilizing its brickwork in the vast mansion he began to raise.

Legend names no architect for Hatfield, but supplies instead the more colourful tale that Salisbury had no architectural aide, buying his drawings for front and rear façades from an outside source and working out the basic necessities for the interstices, as it were, with his clerk on the works, one Thomas Wilson. They must both have had a rare sense of style and worked with a will, for the house was begun in 1607 and completed five years later.

The basic plan was very much of its time; Salisbury was no innovator. He kept to the traditional E-form structure of two wings linked by a central block. Hence, too, the retention of a Great Hall, Long Gallery, Musicians' Gallery, although the plurality of windows was a kind of breakaway foreshadowing those glazed palaces of the Jacobean era. Hatfield is, indeed, a remarkably light and spacious house seen against other great houses of its time. Certainly the house has shown its basic practicality as a Great House, remaining more or less unaltered throughout the 350 years of its existence, an unusual history for any house owned by the English patricians, who have long been numbered amongst the world's most restless changers of the houses they inherit.

The 2nd Earl was the first of a long line of Salisburys to live in the house. He seems to have liked the place, for he spent considerable sums in supervising its finishing touches and then in entertaining, sizably diminishing the family fortune in both activities. He also added the Cecil Chapel to the Parish Church.

The only alterations of note to Hatfield were carried out much later during the eighteenth century when James Wyatt is believed to have been responsible for enlarging the windows in King James' Drawing Room and other rooms.

A disastrous fire, in which the wife of the 7th Earl and 1st Marquess was tragically burned to death, gutted the whole of the West wing in 1835. This was rebuilt by the 2nd Marquess, who also spent vast sums in restoring the house, making possible, in fact, its present-day existence. The 4th Marquess has continued with this family policy of maintaining Hatfield and he has also spent much time, money and study in restoring the house where injudicious alterations had lessened its historical and architectural authenticity.

Opposite *Hatfield House, seen from the garden on the east side*

THE MARQUESS OF SALISBURY is seventy-five, but shows few signs of this lengthy span other than a mildly laborious ascent from a deep-seated armchair. He could pass for a man in his sixties. He is tall, stiff-backed as befits a one-time Grenadier, with silver hair, down-turning military moustache, keen eyes and a liveliness of manner that discounts all legends relating to the magisterial *gravitas* of the Cecils through the centuries. Despite the high offices of State that he has held, he is notably unassuming and relaxed. Even the most rabid egalitarian would find scant trace of any patrician superiority in this man. Indeed, his personal quarters at Hatfield House tot up to fewer rooms than most middle-class households would consider a minimum for a comfortable existence.

'When we are—as normally—alone, my wife and I live in five rooms in this wing,' he explains, sitting deep in one corner of a large sofa. 'A sitting-room and bedroom apiece and a dining-room. Fortunately, the house was built virtually as three houses: this family flat, the east wing for guests and the State Rooms in the central block, which is open to the public.'

The Marquess's sitting-room is also his study: a high, square, panelled room with large sofa, faded loose-covered armchairs and an immense desk set four-square before a vast window overlooking the garden maze and the misted parkland stretching far beyond—'for a mile or so,' the Marquess says casually.

'Has Hatfield always been part of your life?'

Above *The Marquess of Salisbury*
Opposite *The Marble Hall with minstrel's gallery and fine seventeenth-century Brussels tapestries*

'Always. It was my home. I grew up here. I went to school from here. And to Oxford. I also went to the First War from here. So I know it well. So well that when my father died in 'forty-seven it was the most natural thing in the world for me to come back here to take over.'

'Without any kind of trepidation?'

'None of any consequence. I obviously knew it was a big house, but I knew it wouldn't be used as a big house any more. Sixty years ago my father lived over the whole house as a matter of course. He had a large staff. He entertained a good deal. Everything was very different. Now a separate staff looks after the main house which is shown to visitors. We lead quite separate lives in this wing. Things change, but one finds one is curiously resilient in accepting change.'

'How much time do you spend here?'

'Pretty well all the time I don't spend in the Lords. I come down here on Thursday evenings or Friday mornings and go up to London again on Monday afternoons. I get up fairly early, breakfast at nine o'clock and have a daily service in the chapel here.'

'A great part of your life has been concerned with the House of Lords?'

'I suppose one could say that, but not for much longer, I'm afraid, now they've decided to do away with us. Or at least with people like me. But I suppose I'd have to go in any case. I'm getting on and they're going to retire everyone at seventy-two.'

'Unlike most peers you also seem to have had considerable experience in the Commons.'

'Most of my life has been spent in one or the other House. I was elected MP for South Dorset in nineteen-twenty-nine. That's forty years ago this year. I was in the House until nineteen-forty-one. Then Mr Churchill, as he then was, asked me to take over as a minister in the Lords. I soon after became Leader. My father was already there, of course. Indeed, he'd been Leader some years before. But Mr Churchill made me a peer in my own right, by a medieval device which few people know much about, but one which can be very useful on occasion. At least, Mr Churchill thought so on that occasion. My father had what one might call, I suppose, a spare barony and I was created Baron Cecil of Essendon. After my father's death, the title was absorbed once more into my present title.'

'Did you always know you'd take over Hatfield?'

'Almost inevitably. I wanted to, in any case, as does my son, who now manages the estate and comes here once a week from Cranborne in Dorset as I once did. I lived there from the time I married in nineteen-fifteen. We have two houses there: the Manor, where my son lives now, and the Lodge. Many people think the Manor one of the most beautiful small houses in the country. I'm inclined to agree, but perhaps I'm prejudiced. I was very happy there. The Lodge is an eighteenth-century house, pleasant enough, though not so beautiful. But I love the Dorset countryside and usually try to get there two or three times a year. The landscape here is very different.'

'Hatfield, presumably, has changed a good deal during your lifetime.'

'The town certainly has. When I was a boy, Hatfield was little more than a village on our doorstep. Now it's an industrialized town, growing all the time. That's why we are always losing bits of land here and there as it's required for factories, housing and so on.'

'How much land do you have at this moment?'

'Frankly, I'd have to have notice of that question. I couldn't exactly say.'

'And the park?'

'That I can tell you. Sixteen hundred acres, a good deal of which is nowadays farmed. That is quite large, of course. But it is also useful for

Opposite, above *The South Front of Hatfield House, seen through the great gates*
Centre, above *The Maze in the East Garden, laid out about 120 years ago*
Centre, below *The garden on the west side, restored to its original Jacobean form in 1900*
Below *Detail of the tower*

the town, for all residents of Hatfield have, as a matter of tradition, free admission to the park at any time, winter and summer, irrespective of whether the House is open to the public. The park is thus a pretty useful lung for such a swiftly-growing town. We have a system of blue cards for town residents. The lodge-keeper doesn't always demand to see the cards—that would be too much of a good thing—but he does occasionally ask to see them. The system seems to work quite well and, as far as I can tell, isn't abused in any way.'

'Are you personally interested in the estate?'

'I was and I am. I usually try to see my agent every day when I'm here, but of course it's very pleasant for me that my son takes such a practical interest in the place. I'm very fortunate in that we get on well as a family. All that takes an enormous load off one's shoulders. But if my agent wants me to look into something of particular importance, off I go. After all, I've shot over the land for over half-a-century. I know every foot of it pretty well. I don't do much shooting now, but the local knowledge remains.'

'And hunting?'

'This has never been much of a hunting district. Too much wire and now more than ever. I used to ride, but not hunt.'

'Do you mind people coming to Hatfield and wandering around your domain?'

'Not at all. And you have to remember that we're scarcely ever aware that visitors are around. They don't come into this wing or into the part of the garden which you see from this window. So we're very fortunate. And they are very careful as a general rule.'

'The maintenance problems of a large and historic house like this must be pretty formidable.'

'They are indeed. Since the war we've done a great deal of restoration on our own account: repairing stonework, brickwork, the roof and so on. Most of the fabric of the house is original, although we had a disastrous fire here in eighteen-thirty-five when most of the west wing was burned down and the Dowager Lady Salisbury was burned to death. That wing was rebuilt, but none of the brickwork has been touched since. So far we've been able to carry out the work here without asking for any special Government grant. We thought we'd try to pay for it ourselves and so far, by careful planning and budgeting, we've succeeded, step by step. But the middle part of the house will soon need a great deal of attention and that's going to present some very big problems of finance and workmanship to somebody. After all, Robert Cecil began to build the house in sixteen-hundred and seven and had finished it five years later, so it's beginning to be fairly old.'

'Legend says he was his own architect.'

'He seems to have done a good deal himself. It was a remarkable achievement.'

'He and some of your other ancestors have played notable parts in English history. Are their records still here?'

'We've a very large number of Elizabethan letters alone here, including all the manuscripts relating to the building of the house. I'm not an expert in these matters, but I am deeply interested in the subject, which is one reason, I suppose, why I have for years been a member of the Historic Manuscripts Commission and Chairman of the Historical Monuments Commission.'

'Are the records transcribed?'

'Transcribed and issued from time to time in the rather rarefied publications of the Commission.'

'You seem to have been in politics all your life. Do you think Hatfield had its part to play in your choice of a career? Did you ever think of the army, for instance?'

'Never. Although my father, myself and my son all served in the Grenadiers, I never thought of the army as a career, except for the war.'

'Did you train yourself consciously for politics?'

'Not at all in that way. Two of my family had been Chief Ministers of the Crown, and my father was deeply involved in politics all his life. Naturally enough, I suppose, I assumed that I would take an interest in them myself. I didn't speak much in any of the debating societies at Eton or in the Union at Oxford. I suppose I didn't really make my first speech

The Armoury, originally an open portico in the Italian Renaissance style. Much of the armour on the walls was worn by the men of the Spanish Armada

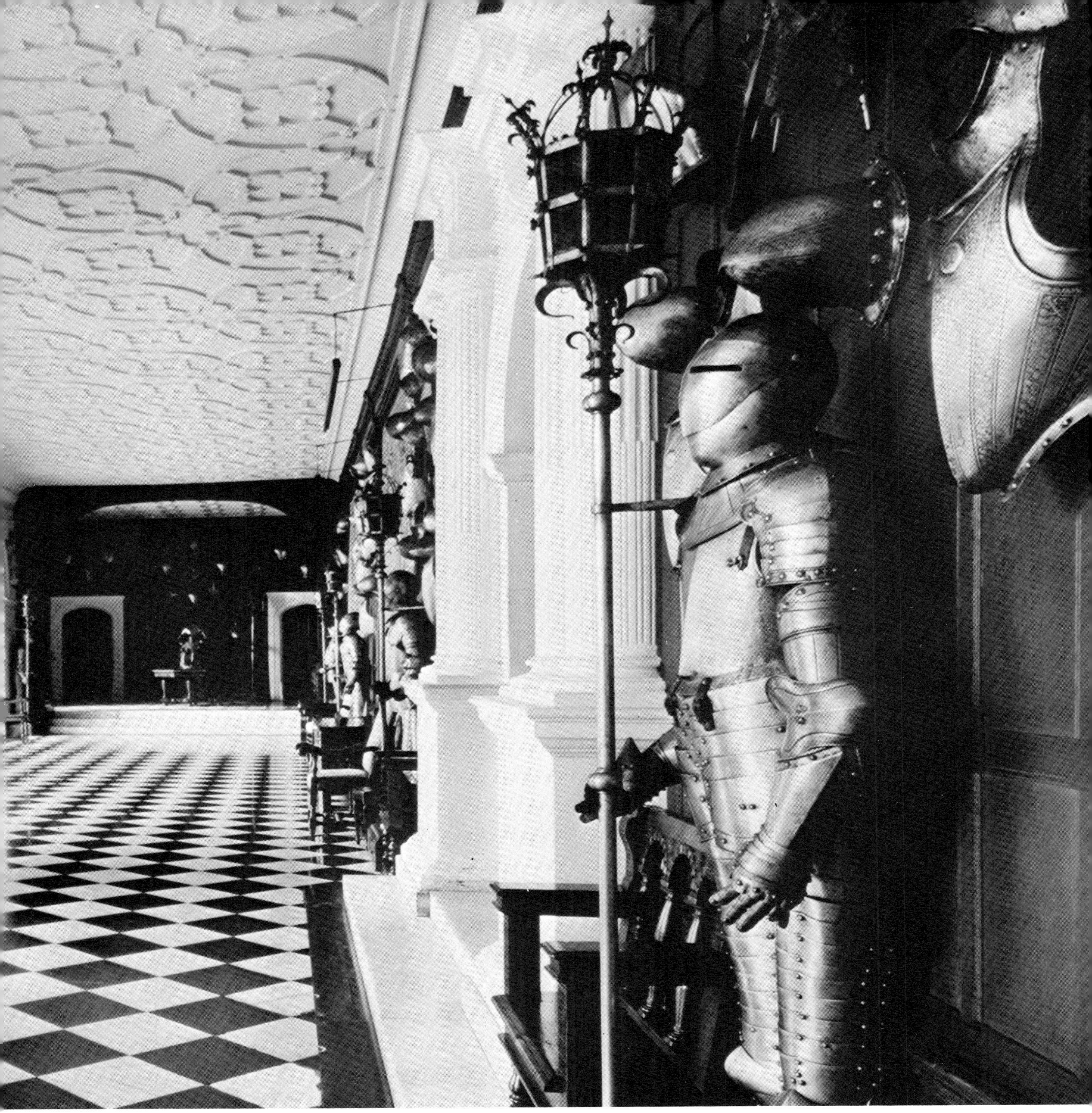

of any consequence until after I entered the House of Commons. I like to think I had served my apprenticeship in other ways. I'd travelled. I'd taken part in a great war. Since then I've been continuously involved in politics in one way or another.'

'For a long time. How long exactly?'

'Well, I've been in the House of Commons or the House of Lords for almost half-a-century and my father had an even longer span. He entered parliament in the early 'eighties of the last century and was active until the mid-nineteen-forties. That's almost a century between the two of us.'

'And your grandfather was Prime Minister.'

'Yes, he was the last of Queen Victoria's Prime Ministers. He must have

Opposite *The elaborately carved oak Grand Staircase with figures surmounting each of the pillars*
Above *The Long Gallery runs the length of the centre of the south front and measures 180 feet*
Below *Another view of the Armoury with the 'Four Seasons' tapestries, woven in 1611*

been a remarkable man: scientist as well as statesman, a member of the Royal Society and so on. Indeed, I think I'm right in saying that thanks to my grandfather's efforts Hatfield was one of the first houses, if not *the* first, in England to be lighted by electricity. He carried out his experiments in the basement under this room. He used to go down by a spiral staircase. I suppose it was a change from Cabinet papers.'

'He also worked in this study?'

'Yes, *he* did. My father didn't. That was his desk, and a very special desk it is, too. He must have had a systematic as well as scientific mind. I don't think the two always go together. He had two slots made in the desk top. Into one—that on the left—his secretary put confidential letters and papers. They fell into a drawer beneath to which only the secretary and my grandfather had keys. When he had time, my grandfather took out the letters from that drawer, drafted replies or made notes and then dropped them through the other slot into the other drawer and locked it: there they awaited his secretary's attention. It's a system of handling confidential letters and papers which could still have lessons for us today.'

'You are generally regarded as the archetypal aristocratic figure of our time. Do you *feel* aristocratic in any way?'

'Not a bit. You must be joking. I think we all feel much the same. We've

Above *The Winter Dining-Room, originally two rooms; the panelled walls are hung with pictures of English kings*
Opposite *The Library with its magnificent chimneypiece by Maximilian Colt and remarkable mosaic of the 1st Earl of Salisbury*

all got work to do.'

'You have a special interest in Rhodesia.'

'We have had for a long time. After all, the capital's called Salisbury, isn't it? It was called after my grandfather: there's a town called Cranborne and another called Hatfield. And we still have a share in two farms there. One begins to shed interests as one gets older, but Rhodesia certainly remains a very active interest of my own.'

'Do you think old age offers any compensations?'

'Oh, yes. Most certainly. Detachment, above all. One doesn't get so worked up or worried over things as one did when one was younger. One tries to cut down one's involvements, but others seem to crop up. Then, too, I've been especially fortunate in my relations with my family. I had three sons. One was killed in the last war, another died at school. But my eldest son and I are close, and I find my grandchildren full of interest. No, old age does have compensations. Would you care to see my grandfather's desk I spoke about?'

With that, the Marquess pulls himself up from the sofa, crosses to the handsome desk that once housed ministerial dockets so secretly and securely and demonstrates the ingenious devices of the desk.

Beyond the window the trees begin to fade in the mists of the late afternoon.

Hatfield

CHARLECOTE PARK

THE LUCY family has been living at Charlecote for many centuries. Reliable records trace the family connexion back to Thurstane de Charlecote upon whom the village was bestowed by Henry de Montford in 1189. But the first Lucy of Charlecote was Thurstane's grandson, Sir William de Lucy, who seems to have adopted the name on his marriage into the family of de Lucy, Lords of Cockermouth in Cumberland.

The present house at Charlecote was begun in 1551 after the old family mansion had been demolished. The builder was a Sir Thomas Lucy, a considerable figure in his time, both commercially and socially, entertaining Queen Elizabeth at Charlecote in 1572. Yet the greater fame of this Sir Thomas derives from a legendary connexion with a Shakespearean poaching expedition, with the playwright-to-be being hauled before Sir Thomas, the resident magistrate. Certainly the portrait of Justice Shallow bears very pointed resemblances to Sir Thomas.

Of the house and its architectural dependencies, the gatehouse is the only building that remains unaltered from the sixteenth century. This small and beautiful feature is a fine example of that transitional period in English architecture which saw gothic and renaissance influences co-existing. Thus the heavy stone gothic vaulting of the arch is partnered by the shell-headed alcoves in the halls, typical of Italian influence.

The house itself was built in the traditional letter-form E, with an octagonal tower at each corner, surmounted by cupola, ball, and weathervane. With its plurality of towers, gables and chimney-stacks the house presents a truly romantic silhouette, its skyline well-matched by the handsome two-storey porch. Unfortunately, certain injudicious additions were made during the last century, although the big oriel window, inserted in the eastern forecourt front of the house by Mary Elizabeth Lucy in the 1830s, is less intrusive than it might have been in less sensitive hands.

The western or river front of the house is, however, almost wholly a Victorian composition, the additions allowing for the introduction of the large dining-room and library. Yet this elevation overlooking the formal gardens, the River Avon and the 200-acre park, has considerable charm thanks to the tall windows and the pierced stone balustrade added in 1858.

To add to the legends which attend this beautiful house, the meadowland seen from these windows is known as the Camp. Here, the story goes, Charles I and his men encamped during the night preceding the Battle of Edgehill in 1642.

The house and park were presented to the National Trust in 1945 by Sir Montgomerie Fairfax-Lucy.

Opposite, above *The Charlecote gatehouse* Below *The entrance front of the E-shaped house, with one of its four octagonal towers*

Major Sir Brian and Lady Fairfax-Lucy
Opposite, above left *The Drawing-Room with walls hung in nineteenth century yellow satin damask. The picture of Charlecote over the chimney-piece was painted in 1696*
Right *The Tapestry Room with highback chairs in ebony inlaid with ivory*
Below left *The Dining-Room, showing the massive Victorian sideboard in carved oak by Willcox*
Right *The Library has bookcases and woodwork also carved by Willcox*

For most natives and not a few foreigners Charlecote Park would seem to be the perfect English Stately Home with its compact and beautiful house set within a compact and beautiful park. To which is added one of the most enduring of English legends.

The setting of Charlecote in the plain of the Warwickshire Avon is idyllic with the River Avon and a tributary, the Hele, meandering through the pleasantly undulating parkland.

The house and gatehouse are approached from a lane, six miles south of Warwick, four miles east of Stratford-on-Avon, between the village of Hampton Lucy and the hamlet of Charlecote. A short avenue of elms leads to the gatehouse: a majestic avenue of limes lies beyond.

The gatehouse is perhaps Charlecote's major visual delight, setting the house at once in its historical context. This little building is like a delicate and entrancing toy fort made by Renaissance craftsmen: a foursquare building with stone balustrading and octagonal tower capped with ogival cupolas, a gay sixteenth-century interpretation of the military architecture of more martial earlier times. Nowadays, its brickwork has mellowed to an elusive rosy-pink, enhanced by the grey stone dressings.

The visitor passes through the forecourt, enclosed by the old stable buildings, brew-house and brick walls, to the house, greatly altered from the original Elizabethan structure.

Much of the house, exterior and interior, is Victorian. The bay windows, for instance, were built in 1853, and the vast oriel window of the Great Hall is also Victorian reconstruction. Some of the alterations would undoubtedly sadden an architectural purist, but for most visitors the house still retains much of its Tudor atmosphere, thanks mainly to the fact that a great deal of the original brickwork survives and to the still romantic appeal of the facade with its many gables, grouped chimney-stacks and octagonal towers standing at the four corners of the house, each surmounted by cupola, ball and weathervane.

The two-storeyed porch, protecting a doorway flanked by Ionic pilasters supporting coupled Corinthian columns, is an original feature, which is as well, for it dominates the front of the house facing the visitor arriving in the courtyard. Above the doorway are the arms of Queen Elizabeth added by Sir Thomas Lucy, supposedly in honour of an expected royal visit.

There could scarcely be two greater contrasts in setting than the fore-court facade of Charlecote and the river front, which retains far more of the original fabric, having received far less attention from Victorian Lucys. A formal garden leads to the Avon which is reached by a flight of stone steps. The meadowland on the opposite bank is known as The Camp and tradition has it that the army of Charles I was encamped here the night before the Battle of Edgehill, but the mind's eye of a visitor is more likely to see this Warwickshire arcadia peopled by gallants and their ladies engaged in their sylvan pleasures than warriors preparing for battle.

A more tenacious tradition than that relating to The Camp encompasses Charlecote, for it was here, in this parkland, legend says, that Shakespeare, as a young man of Stratford-on-Avon, was caught on a poaching expedition and was hauled before Sir Thomas Lucy, resident magistrate, in the Great Hall of Charlecote and received whatever punishment was his due. Substance is given to the legend by the playwright's waspish portrait of Justice Shallow in *Henry IV* (Part II) and in the *Merry Wives of Windsor*, which has more than a passing likeness to what is known of Sir Thomas. Shakespeare's reference to the 'dozen white luces' in Shallow's coat of arms seems rather more pointed than a casual coincidence would have occasioned.

The Lucys have lived at Charlecote since the twelfth century. A Thurstane de Charlecote was given the village by Henry de Montford in 1189. His grandson, Sir William de Lucy, who, it is presumed, took the name of his wife, daughter of a baronial family of that name in Cumberland, was the first Lucy of Charlecote. But it was a later de Lucy, the first Sir Thomas, who pulled down the buildings which then stood at Charlecote and began to build the present house in 1551.

In 1945, Sir Montgomerie Fairfax-Lucy gave Charlecote to the National Trust: two hundred acres of parkland, house and contents, including pictures and a notable library of over three thousand volumes, many of historic importance.

Today, his brother, Major Sir Brian Fairfax-Lucy, wanders through the park at Charlecote, talking frankly about the problems and inevitable regrets and heartache involved in having one's ancestral home in the care of others, however well-intentioned.

Sir Brian is scarcely the usual idea of a regular soldier. He is of above middle height and, with his strong-boned, clean-shaven face and deep-set eyes, looks far more the author he is than the soldier he was. Yet he saw service in two world wars and on the North-West Frontier between wars. He has written five children's books, including *Horse in the Valley* and *The Horse from India*, and, more recently, *Children of the House*, all of which have proved extremely popular. He is married to the only daughter of another author, the first Lord Tweedsmuir, who, although he was an outstandingly successful Governor-General of Canada, remained always better known as John Buchan, author of *The Thirty-Nine Steps*, the evergreen *Greenmantle* and historical studies of Augustus and Cromwell.

'People often think that giving one's ancestral home to the National Trust brings in a lot of advantages,' he says. 'But the picture isn't quite as rosy as all that. Far from it. I know it's a widely-held fallacy that giving your home to the National Trust entitles you to live in it free of financial worries. This is no more true than to think it's easy to get the Trust to take your house. When it appears in the Press that So-and-So has presented the Trust with his ancestral mansion and estates, it conjures a picture of the owner handing over the title-deed with a lordly gesture and thereafter being "kept up" in the hereditary state to which he has been accustomed.'

'What are the cold facts, then?'

'The cold facts, as you say, are that the Trust do not accept properties that are not adequately endowed, and the owner, if he chooses to remain as a tenant, pays full rates and upkeep on his quarters. In nineteen-forty-five the endowment asked for Charlecote was twenty thousand pounds. It would now be four times as much. Crippled by death duties we were unable to find the money for an endowment. Instead we gave over two hundred acres of parkland with two large herds of deer, Spanish sheep and the entire contents of the house, gold plate, pictures, library and so on. It was accepted and was, I believe, the only property to be taken without an endowment as well.'

'What arrangements did you come to with the Trust about your own living-quarters? Surely that can be a tricky point?'

'A hundred and thirty years ago my great-grandfather built on a wing with nurseries, kitchens and servants' quarters. When, as head of the family, I became tenant-for-life under the National Trust I was allotted this wing for my family's use. We accepted the limitations of our new quarters and turned the butler's pantry into a kitchen, gladly making the

best of the half-loaf. Some years later a curator was housed in one wing of the main house and a flat for a caretaker has since been converted from the rooms where the lamps and boots used to be cleaned.'

'What about the upkeep of the grounds?'

'For the sake of economy, the formal garden was put back to grass. The staff that now runs Charlecote is composed of a curator, a caretaker, a park-keeper and one gardener.'

'Surely it was all rather a traumatic experience?'

'Well, frankly it was. But, curiously enough, what were even more difficult to bear were the doubts cast by visiting picture and furniture experts on the value of heirlooms which we had taken for granted. The old Servants' Hall in our wing, which, fortunately, happened to be fairly roomy, was filled up with their throw-outs. All this was over twenty years ago, of course. Since then, a new generation of experts has grown up. Many of our denigrated pictures have been restored to critical favour and given places of honour. Taste changes and experts disagree—and we have watched this happening with some wry amusement. But, in the process, the rooms have become sadly de-humanized, which is apt to happen when all signs of family occupation are banished.'

'What about the period of adjustment? Wasn't that fairly painful occasionally?'

'The first five years were, inevitably, a difficult period for both sides. Fortunately, we were helped and advised by James Lees-Milne, then Historic Buildings Secretary to the Trust. But there was no direct contact with the Central Committee. The then-Lord Esher, for instance, king-pin of the Trust at the time, only paid us one brief visit. The one really sympathetic member of the Trust was Harold Nicolson, not knighted then. He came over to Charlecote with his wife. It happened to be the day on which the BBC was broadcasting a programme on the work of the Trust which included a scene which I had recorded for them of the ceremony of handing over the keys of Charlecote to the Chairman of the Trust. It was a cold day and we sat in the housekeeper's room where there was a fire and listened to the wireless. The broadcast included the sound of rooks cawing in the elms and the chiming of the gatehouse clock, and the voice of our old keeper lamenting in a broad Warwickshire dialect the passing of the "old gentry." Tears rolled down Nicolson's cheeks—it was the greatest, if not the happiest, compliment I've ever had.'

'After those early experiences how, would you say, has the arrangement worked out?'

'In a quickly-changing world gentlemen's agreements are as nebulous and as difficult to carry out as is a marriage contract. In this case the spirit of the bargain has been honoured on both sides. We have accepted inevitable changes inside and out, and on the whole the Trust has asked our approval before making such changes. Successive "new brooms" have suggested introducing white deer into the park, allowing camping sites, and canoes on the Avon. At one point pressure was brought to bear on us to allow our wing to be demolished, but family sentiment was respected and, at least for the time being, the project has been dropped.'

'Any real contretemps?'

'Well, I wasn't able to prevent the felling of eleven walnut trees planted by Capability Brown to clear a temporary deficit in the budget, or the cutting down of the box and yew hedges which were part of Brown's scheme for the Wilderness. And where it has been a case of pressing necessity, like replacing gates or replanting trees, I have met the Trust officials with cap in one hand and cheque-book in the other, for it is only too true that most of their properties exceed the yearly estimate for their

Opposite above *A stone figure of a shepherd in the garden*
Centre *The East Front entrance*
Bottom *Gateway and avenue of limes leading to Charlecote House*

upkeep, owing to rising costs. All this has to be done formally through the proper channel, on the lines of a complaint from a junior officer to the Army Council.'

'Do you mind people walking through your home as if somebody else owned it?'

'This is too complex to be answered simply. When we gave the house to the National Trust we knew we were parting with four hundred years of family life, and that we'd never again be free to enjoy it in the same way. This was the price we had to pay for retaining our connexion with Charlecote where the Lucys have lived for nearly eight hundred years.'

'And presumably for another eight hundred years?'

'Who knows? Nominally, I'm tenant-for-life of the wing we use, but there's no guarantee that my son will succeed me here as tenant. I often feel as much of a stranger here as the visitors who wander through the gardens. The State rooms are like museums. All traces of family tenancy have been swept away.'

'Do you still remember much of the old way of life?'

'These things fade. I now have difficulty in recalling what tea in the Library in summer was like. Or a dinner-party with the gold plate in the big dinner room. No table laid for a meal that is never going to be eaten can give anything like the impression of boundless hospitality which prevailed at Charlecote in my mother's early days here. Chairs and sofas set stiffly about an empty fireplace can never evoke the atmosphere of tea-parties. All the same, I'm delighted if visitors do carry away happy impressions, and if the more imaginative ones are able to picture the Drawing-Room lit with oil lamps and candles, when my mother and her sisters used to sing to the now-silent harp, so much the better.'

'What is your main reaction to visitors?'

'Well, I can truthfully say that I do like to see parents and children enjoying the garden, and lingering on a summer's evening until the last moment before the gates are closed. But it does distress me to see the deterioration of the house. Now we get as many people walking over its floors in the course of one season as we did in four hundred years. This is merely one problem of these historic houses and their future to which the Trust will have to find a solution.'

'What is your greatest regret about handing over the house?'

'As one grows older, I suppose, one prizes privacy above all other forms of self-indulgent luxury, but once your house and garden are open to the public for six days out of the seven throughout the greater part of the year you can no longer expect to enjoy this luxury. Not that I'm complaining. In the winter I can, if I want to, wander with a gun along the deserted river-bank and come back to a silent house peopled by ghosts.'

'Meantime, presumably, maintenance is a major problem?'

'Terrifying. That is perhaps the hardest to bear. The constant reminder that, in spite of the visitors who pour through all the time, Charlecote is always "in the red." The rising cost of keeping roofs, chimneys, windows in sound repair are a ceaseless problem for the Trust. Another is that the central heating of rooms that were never meant to be heated causes rapid decay in old furniture. Of course one wants to be warm, but that is the price of comfort. I'm fully aware of the difficulties of maintenance that confront the Trust's area agents, and they shouldn't be minimized. The public has come to take "Stately Homes" for granted, and I should like to make a plea to all who spend their holiday afternoons in sightseeing of this kind to remember not only the vigilance of the Trust officials who guard their upkeep, but the invisible one-time owners for whom these houses not long ago were homes.'

Above *The coach-house containing various carriages used by the Lucy family throughout the nineteenth century*
Opposite *The Great Hall at Charlecote has been considerably altered from its original appearance. The ornamental marble table-top came from the Borghese Palace in Rome via the Fonthill sale in 1823*

LONGLEAT HOUSE

LONGLEAT, one of the most beautiful and, in the words of Sir John Summerson, one of the 'prodigy' houses of Elizabeth's reign, was also one of the most complicated in its building. Four Longleats were built, the first in 1547, the last in 1572. They were built by Sir John Thynne, one of those tough and thrusting Elizabethans, with a passion for money-making and building.

In its final form, Longleat was the first house in this country that could truthfully be termed a Renaissance house, symbol of Thynne's ambitions and tribute to two remarkable men, each a stonemason and carver of high skill, between whom Mark Girouard,* a leading authority on Longleat, is inclined to divide the responsibility for the design of the building, although he does not discount considerable influence from the owner.

The earlier versions of Longleat had been built of local stone, but the Longleat we see now was built of the finest Bath stone, with Thynne himself probably watching over every detail of the operation, from the shipping of the stone to the hiring and firing of men.

The exterior of Longleat is remarkable in its time, above all for its surprising symmetry in an age of asymmetrical elevations, which more accurately typified the highly individual, extrovert, assertive Elizabethan *persona.* All four sides, magnificently windowed, make Longleat a glittering Tudor palace, unlike any house of its time in England, or, for that matter, in Europe.

The interior of Longleat has a less coherent story. The original main staircase was replaced by one reputedly designed by Sir Christopher Wren, which was, in turn, superseded by the present staircase designed in 1800 by Sir Jeffry Wyatville, who was also responsible for the rooftop cupola. The Saloon was originally the Long Gallery, and has important additions made in the last decades of the nineteenth century, notably the chimney piece which is a copy of one in the Doge's Palace. The State Drawing Room, too, owes a sizable debt to Venice, for the ceiling of that splendid room is copied from that of the library of St Mark's Cathedral.

The gardens of Longleat have also had their vicissitudes. The rural simplicity of Sir John Thynne's original gardens was later replaced by the 1st Lord Weymouth with formal parterres, statues, fountains and other fashionable gardening motifs. These gardens were neglected by his son, who, when he died in 1751, left a wilderness. Capability Brown was brought in. The remains of the formal gardens were swept away and the existing series of lakes and the waterfall were introduced. The park as it is today remains, at heart, a Capability Brown masterpiece, although the post-war years have seen much necessary replanning under the care of Russell Page, the eminent landscape gardener, and the present Marquess.

Opposite *The splendid Tudor roofline of Longleat*

* *Robert Smythson and the Architecture of the Elizabethan Era.* By Mark Girouard (Country Life. 1966)

Left *The Marquess of Bath with his wife and daughter, Silvy, in the Library*
Opposite *Approach view of the East Front*

FOUR MILES out of Warminster, on the A362 to Frome, you come on the modest entrance to Longleat, easily overlooked. No great arches. No colonnade set athwart the highway. Merely a modest indication that Longleat is within.

A momentary touch of confusion is permissible and understandable for another sign, lettered blue-on-white, says TO THE LION RESERVE, and indicates straight on.

Those, less intrepid than others, pressing on, take the Longleat entrance and soon begin to realize that the drive is perhaps longer than they had anticipated—and more splendid. Indeed, the approach to Longleat must be one of the longest and most magnificently-timbered introductions to any house in Britain, with natives and exotics, deciduous and conifers, equally abundant.

The drive continues: utterly quiet, wholly entrancing, oddly deceptive, for, suddenly, after a mile or so of this woodland idyll the track opens out to the edge of a gentle escarpment and there, half-a-mile away, down in a valley all its own, is Longleat, one of the most beautiful houses in the

Opposite *The Great Hall, with hunting-scenes and armorial bearings, has seen little change since 1580*
Above *The Saloon, originally the Long Gallery, with Flemish wall tapestries and massive chimney piece*

world: a tawny-coloured palatial toy with a plurality of glinting windows topped by fanciful turrets, pinnacles and other skyline ornaments, a house which has been called by a scholar, the 'sudden efflorescence of splendour that ushered in the great age of Elizabethan architecture.'

The felicitous shock of Longleat is sudden and complete. No matter how often the visitor has seen pictures of the house the reality is more beautiful. Like Venice, it lives up to all expectation, surpasses all anticipation.

The road winds slowly down to the courtyard, and the house, far more austere, far bigger than it seems from the hillside.

Even at ten-thirty in the morning the crowds are already there, the car-park filling up.

Standing in the library, which houses one of the finest private book collections in the western world, Henry Thynne, sixth Marquess of Bath, seems ready-made to match up to any Hollywood casting specification for an upper-crust Englishman. Tall, dark, handsome, with outdoor looks, a lively step, and looking far, far younger than his sixty-odd years. But after that initial matching the casting outline begins to blur, for he is the least pompous of men, wearing his lineage as lightly as a lambswool pullover, restless and eager to get on with the job in hand. He is racily articulate, worldly-wise, quick to laughter and bang-up-to-the-minute in his appreciation of Britain's vast social changes. His personal grip, and stamp, on one of today's toughest tycoonish tasks—keeping his beautiful house at the top of the Stately Homes League—has made him a legend in his own time.

He is a man of considerable energy and wholly lacking in any touch of self-importance. He lives in the present and plainly enjoys the experience. That he grew up in the house, knows every rod, pole and perch of its surrounding ten thousand acres and now sees almost a quarter-of-a-million strangers a year wandering through his domain, doesn't depress him a bit. He loves Longleat but with a curious detachment that makes his extraordinary forays into showmanship wholly unexpected to friends and competitors alike.

But he sees no inconsistency in his affection for a beautiful house and his welcome to those many unknown visitors. He manages, with the greatest of ease, to fuse the two polarities.

'I couldn't keep it going off my own bat,' he says candidly. 'I'm not that rich. In fact I imagine there aren't more than half-a-dozen families in Britain who could keep a place like this going on their own, with never an outside soul visiting them.'

'But do you really like having quite so many visitors?'

'I don't get to know 'em, so I can't say I like 'em or dislike 'em. The main thing is I need visitors. You mightn't realize it—how could you?—but Longleat, I'm told, will need eight thousand a year for the next ten years to cope with woodworm alone. It sounds a high figure. It did to me. But it's what the experts say it'll cost and I have to take their figures. And they're checked. The Government pays a sizable whack of the repair bill and the officially-appointed architect makes pretty frequent and searching visits here. Finding that kind of money needs people coming here in crowds. And it's only fair and reasonable to see that they get their money's worth when they get here. To start with they can get a snack. Did you know you can't get a cup of tea at Chatsworth?' he adds with an amused smile.

'Did you enjoy growing up here?'

'I did. A lot. It was lonely and I was only here during school holidays. There were seven of us. My parents, elder brother and my three sisters. My brother would have inherited, of course, but he was killed in the First War, in nineteen-fifteen. I was ten at the time and the realization that I'd have to run Longleat came as rather a shock. I'd never even thought of it as likely to be mine.'

'Did you ever think you'd keep it going as a private house?'

'Fortunately, one never takes all that kind of thing in at that age. But somehow, remotely maybe, I suppose I thought I would.'

'How *had* you thought of Longleat?'

'Mainly as a home, but I also knew its great days were over. Even at that age I knew that, basically, Longleat was a relic. After all, it's a house where one entertained one's friends in rather a grand way. Those days are gone. It was originally built way back in the sixteenth century by Sir John as a place in which to show off and entertain his friends—although he never lived to do it—but I suppose its greatest days were in my grandfather's time.

Opposite above left *The State Dining-Room with leather-covered walls, painted ceiling, Wyatville fireplace and Italian overmantel*
Right *The King's Bedroom. The portrait of Prince Henry, elder son of James I, over the fireplace is attributed to Zucchero*
Below, left *The green Library, containing part of the extensive Longleat collection*
Right *The Bishop Ken Library houses a fine collection of children's books and Churchilliana*
Above *Royal mementos in a corner of the library*

He was a great host and the place must have been at its best then—as a late Victorian house and home.'

'Did your parents try to keep it up between the wars?'

'My father and mother kept it up on a much reduced scale, but after my mother died in nineteen twenty-seven, my father lost heart, entertained less and less and the household staff became almost negligible. Although he did virtually nothing to the inside of the house, he maintained the structure and roof which, of course, are the basic essentials in preserving any house.'

'What happened to Longleat during the war?'

'We were fortunate. It was taken over by a girls' school so we didn't suffer as much as other houses like this. Nevertheless, when I came back from the war I found it a pretty daunting prospect, and when my father died in nineteen forty-six, I knew we'd have to do something and so I opened it to the public in 'forty-nine—incidentally, the first house ever to be opened to the public on a thorough-going commercial basis.'

'Do you run the whole enterprise now?'

'I suppose I do, but nobody can run this kind of enterprise on his own. I have colleagues and damned useful they are. I don't, for instance, know a thing about lions.'

'But you do like having the lions around?'

'They're interesting. And so are the chimpanzees.'

'Did you have any part in . . . collecting . . . them?'

'Ninety per cent is my partner, Jimmy Chipperfield's work. He's virtually the boss. After all, he's grown up in the circus world. He knows most of what there is to know about lions. He also knows where to find 'em, which is quite a point; how to tell good from bad; how they should be looked after and all that. But my wife and I did personally go to Ethiopia last year and bought a dozen belonging to the "Lion of Judah" himself. They're now in the Reserve.'

'And where did your partner find the others?'

'In zoos, mostly. In France, Germany, Ireland. We find the zoo types better. House-trained, so to speak. We've had a couple of ex-circus types but they don't seem to get on so well with the others.'

'And they've been a sound investment?'

'I should say so. They've not only kept the figures up, but have raised the house attendance by eighty per cent. People obviously like driving through the Reserve. They must do. After all, it costs 'em a quid a carload, no matter how many in the car, and the figures keep rising, so presumably they enjoy the experience and tell their friends.'

'How many Longleat lions are there now?'

'We've got about thirty, but it's a biggish reserve and I think we need sixty. We could certainly accommodate 'em. One doesn't want 'em to be too thin on the ground. That's the figure we're aiming for, anyway, and hope to achieve this year.'

'I know you don't live here, but do you come here every day?'

'I usually put in an appearance here every day. I think one must. If the chap at the top gets slack it goes right down the line. In any case, I thoroughly enjoy coming here.'

'Could you outline an average day in your life?'

'Well, as you probably know, we live about four miles away. I usually get up about half-past seven, read the post and then have breakfast. Then around nine I drive into Warminster where I have my own office and dictate my letters—it's only a mile away. Then my day begins. I usually come over here later and see how things are going. Then I'm apt to shoot off to the trees, as it were. We have about five thousand acres of woodland here and forestry's my special interest. I usually aim to spend at least three half-

Opposite, above and centre *Roof sculpture and towers at Longleat*
Below *One of the visitors' boats on the lake*

days a week in the woods. We run it as a business and there's a lot of work to do, what with felling, growing, milling and selling the timber.'

'Are you interested in trees apart from their marketing possibilities?'

'Heavens, yes. They're a hobby of mine. For instance, I'm trying to grow an avenue of tulip trees here, which I believe to be the largest in the world—it contains a hundred-and-eighty-four trees. A devilishly difficult tree to grow as you may know. But we seem to be winning. At the beginning I was losing about twelve a year, but I've reduced that considerably. They're twelve feet high now. I cross my fingers and think we'll make it.

'Longleat seems unusually well-equipped as a tourist attraction.'

'Well, it's only fair, isn't it? Most of 'em come a long way to get here and the least one can do is to see that they can spend a decent day here. That's why I take a special interest in the so-called amenities. Sufficient and efficient lavatories, for instance. It's very important. If you're in business, you're in business.'

'What are your latest innovations?'

'Well, we've got two brand new boats for the lake which encircles the island where the chimpanzees live. They're pretty impressive craft I can tell you. As fine as I could get. These cost two thousand guineas apiece. One's named after my nine-year-old daughter, Silvy, and the other after Jimmy's daughter, Mary. We launched them the other day. That's why Silvy is wearing that nautical rig. She got that as her part of the celebrations.'

'Do you ever have any regrets when you see the crowds wandering around that you can't keep it up as a private house?'

'Not really. I have never lived in Longleat after my first marriage, which was in nineteen twenty-seven. My own house—Job's Mill, which you've shown in your magazine—is now what I'm accustomed to. More the kind of country house that any sensible person wants to live in these days. But Longleat is still my first love.'

'What about your wife?'

'Well, she loves Longleat, but not to live in. I think she gets a bit starry-eyed thinking of me as a little chap wandering downstairs with a candle at midnight going to get an apple, or letting my dog out. Apart from that, she's too fond of the Mill.'

'Have you ever entertained here at all?'

'From time to time. We've had the occasional party. But it's hard work. There's no kitchen in operation here now, of course. Everything has to be brought in. It's not an experience any sane man wants to repeat very often!'

'Does anyone actually live here?'

'My eldest son lives here. In a corner of the place, of course. He's an artist. He's apt to divide his life between here and swinging Chelsea. Longleat seems to suit him.'

'Will he keep Longleat open to the public?'

'Who knows? Does one ever know about one's children? Probably. It's difficult to see how Longleat could go on without public support. In any case, I don't see how one can keep this kind of place to oneself any more. The world has changed. Anyway, I shan't be around. It won't be my concern any more.'

With that the Marquess strides across to the window. Outside, the tourists are really beginning to crowd the courtyard, waiting to join the groups assembling under the genial directions of the guides. More cars are coming down through the woods.

Longleat's owner watches them all with an indulgent smile. Apparently without regret. He is that rarest of birds: a twentieth-century man with a sixteenth-century palace on his hands and thoroughly enjoying the problems of keeping up with the Government.

LEIXLIP CASTLE

LEIXLIP CASTLE is built on a commanding position at the meeting of the Rivers Ryewater and Liffey, above the famous Salmon Leap, from which the name is derived, for the area was once a Danish settlement christened *Lax-hlaup* i.e. Salmon Leap. The leap is now, alas, submerged by an electric dam, and, as all place-names in Ireland are now recorded in Irish, Leixlip has been literally translated as *Leim an Bhradain*, leap of the salmon.

According to that rich source-book, *The Castles of Ireland*, compiled by C. L. Adams over sixty years ago, Leixlip Castle is generally supposed to have been built by the De Hereford family towards the close of the twelfth century, on land given to Adam de Hereford by Strongbow after the Norman landing at Wexford in 1169.

The present building consists of two blocks set at right angles, facing east and south. The east wing probably incorporates part of the twelfth-century keep, and with the north-east circular tower represents the oldest portion of the structure, although now pierced by comparatively modern windows. In this part of the Castle is a room in which, legend affirms, King John slept during his stay in Ireland.

By the end of the thirteenth century Leixlip had passed to the Pypard family, and in 1302 the castle and its lands were surrendered to the King, and after various ownerships and vicissitudes, the Castle was named, in 1494, as one of the Irish fortresses that could only have an Englishman as its Constable.

The castle passed into the care of various owners, but, owing to its proximity to Dublin and its commanding position, was invariably apt to be a centre of plot and counterplot until well into the seventeenth century.

In 1732 Leixlip was bought by William Conolly, speaker of the Irish House of Commons, but, as Castletown was his principal seat, the Castle once more reverted to a varied list of owners and tenants, starting with Conolly's nephew before passing out of that family in 1914.

According to the enquiries of the present owner, Leixlip seems to have been modernized in what he terms 'a reasonably civilized sense' in the first half of the eighteenth century, judging by the cornices and panelling. The gothick windows also have the solid generous proportions and heavy glazing bars of the mid-century.

Opposite *The Castle seen at the junction of the River Liffey and Rye Water*

DESMOND GUINNESS and his wife are kept so busy preserving the architecture of Georgian Ireland that it would seem, to the outsider, that they can scarcely have any time to themselves at home.

They spend their time travelling from one end of Ireland to the other, giving advice on restoration, finding uses for unwanted buildings and so on. They are also at war with the speculators in, and desecrators of, Dublin's Georgian squares and terraces. Mr. Guinness spends a sizable part of the year lecturing in the United States on the architectural treasures and pleasures of Ireland. He has also dipped deeply into his own personal fortune (to the tune of £97,000) to save Castletown, the most impressive Georgian house in Ireland, from development and whatever other horrors that over-comfortably reassuring word can too often mean. Now Castletown is the headquarters of the Irish Georgian Society and Mr. Guinness and his fellow-members are spending much of their time, energies and money in seeking to sustain the house against the ravages of time, climate and general apathy. Much of the work there is done by volunteers, out of love for the house.

For their own home, Desmond Guinness, a lively-minded, energetic, handsome man in his late thirties, and his wife, have chosen a somewhat earlier house than one built in the Georgian era. No less than an Irish castle overlooking the racing River Liffey and the village of Leixlip, eleven miles outside Dublin.

'To a visitor Leixlip seems a particularly pleasant place to live in, made-to-measure for any romantic. A castle. Modernized. Not too large, not too small and extremely comfortable.'

'We certainly find it so, and I do see what you mean about the romantic part. The murmur of the river, the beat of swans flying overhead, wind and rain shaking the very fabric of the castle when there's a storm—these are the sounds we live by. Even after ten years we still appreciate them.'

'What was it like when you came here?'

'Very different from now, I assure you. The bathtubs had been put out-of-doors for the cattle to drink from, and, conversely, the farm had found its way indoors. After moving into our own bedroom we found written on the wallpaper: "Nineteen-fifty-five Oats, twenty-seven Sacks". It seems a lifetime ago.'

'Everything had to be done from scratch, presumably?'

'Everything. From the roof downwards. Even the electricity had been disconnected. In Ireland the current is always switched off when a house changes hands and stays switched off until the wiring is considered safe. My wife moved in with a gun and a cat, and slept surrounded by books in a room on the ground floor; I was away at the time.'

'When was all this?'

'That was in May, nineteen-fifty-eight. We should have had possession earlier, in February, but the previous owner couldn't be persuaded to budge—so we more or less besieged him. Even then he tried to bribe us not to buy Leixlip, but finally he let us have the land, which we started to farm. We then planted trees outside the windows. After all, it was meant to be ours by this time. The day he told us not to make a bonfire as it would spoil the grass we began to wonder if Leixlip would ever belong to us.'

'Is it true to say that Guinness Stout was born in Leixlip?'

'The village of Leixlip is steeped in Guinness tradition. Archbishop Price, who died in seventeen-fifty-two and is buried in our church, left

one hundred pounds to 'his servant, Richard Guinness,' and a further hundred pounds to Richard's son, Arthur. The will is preserved in Trinity College. Tradition has it that he also left a secret recipe for brewing a very dark beer. In any case, Richard Guinness set up his brewery on the main street of Leixlip, and in seventeen-fifty-nine Arthur started to brew in Dublin, eleven miles farther along the River Liffey. Archbishop Price, by the way, was responsible for what I always consider the greatest architectural crime yet committed in Ireland. He deliberately took the roof off the great Romanesque cathedral on the Rock of Cashel, which, even as a ruin, is the finest example we have of the period. To anyone interested in archaeology or architecture that's pretty well equivalent to the desecration of the Acropolis, an equally unnecessary act. Perhaps, in some small way, we're atoning for the Archbishop's misdeed by organizing as we do, a society dedicated to the preservation of eighteenth-century buildings in Ireland.'

'That presumably is your Irish Georgian Society?'

'Yes. The society is run from Castletown, a magnificent Palladian house only three miles from Leixlip, and which belonged for two hundred years to the Conollys who also owned Leixlip Castle. It is the only great house near Dublin that is open to the public. We publish a quarterly journal on all aspects of the eighteenth-century arts in Ireland which is sent to the six thousand members. Our subscription is two pounds a year and we badly need more members. By stimulating an intelligent interest in the period we hope to encourage the preservation of the best of the past for the future.'

'Leixlip must have been somewhat daunting to start furnishing after the vicissitudes you've described.'

'It was rather. The most difficult thing was to find furniture large enough not to be dwarfed by the high dados that go round most of the rooms. It's a popular misconception that you can buy large things cheaply "because nobody wants them". I suppose when people say that kind of thing they're thinking of those carved oak dressers like the one my Oxford landlady was so fond of: she often used to tell us what a lot of work there was in it! My wife went to auction after auction. But she's a highly individual and compulsive buyer. She would set out with the firm conviction that she was off to buy something useful like a table or a chair, but she usually came home with an Irish elk, a suit of armour or a case of stuffed birds. We've been collecting shells for so long now that they've found their way into every room. Not that I mind: they're far more beautiful than anything made by the hand of man.'

'Is Leixlip actually big or small? It's always difficult to tell with castles, whether in Spain or Scotland—or Ireland.'

'Well, as you probably know, there wasn't much puritan modesty in sponsors of eighteenth-century building in Ireland. Their houses were meant for show. To make the façade even more impressive all sorts of stables and outbuildings would be pressed into service.'

'Were the battlements also eighteenth-century adornments by the unpuritanical owners of the time?'

'Oddly enough, no. The battlements, for instance, don't appear on eighteenth-century engravings. They were probably added by George Cavendish, the tenant in the early nineteenth century. By that time it was once more fashionable to live in a castle. Indeed, the prosperity that Napoleon's blockade brought to our agriculture resulted in a great rash of mock embattled castles—like Pakenham and Birr. Those who could not afford to rebuild would add gothick crenellations to the unsuspecting Georgian house—ominous leaks would be sure to appear—or merely

Opposite, above *Mr. Desmond Guinness with his two children Patrick and Marina*
Below *The white-painted Gothick door opens off a dark-green, stone-flagged hall*

content themselves with a grand set of gothick gates. The word 'castle' is used in Ireland to describe a classical house. "Above at the castle", one often hears somebody say, referring to some square Regency box. It's rather as in France the word "chateau" has a double meaning. It seemed to suit the pretensions of the Anglo-Irish to live in a castle, but usually such so-called castles are far smaller than they appear to be. Leixlip is the very opposite. There are, in fact, more rooms than one could possibly imagine. Most of them of peculiar shapes and sizes that fortunately lend themselves to unusual schemes of decoration and furnishing.'

'You seem to have taken up the challenge.'

'In a way it was inevitable. Being interested in these matters and being the second of a family of eleven, I had nothing of my own so we had to furnish Leixlip from scratch. Our children have an enormous doll's house, which they use as a toy-cupboard, the front door being suspended in mid-air with practical drawers below it. It came from a house designed by Richard Castle, the German architect who practised in Ireland in the eighteenth century. We think it was designed by him. The Brighton Pavilion bed was bought at an auction at Fawley Court with a view to its going to the Pavilion, but it was rejected and came to us instead. The Regency barrel organ that stands in the Gothick Room plays "Rule Britannia" and "God Save the Queen," sedition nicely counter-balanced by "The Harp That Once".'

'And the splendidly colourful decoration?'

'My wife decorated the yellow bedroom with any old blue-and-white china plates, dishes and jars that she could find so that it looks like a sort of juggler's nightmare, and the bed-hangings are blue-and-white to match. The staircase walls were painted an orange colour copied from Malahide Castle, which has, in turn, been copied by several of our friends. As there are so many grey days in Ireland we've used a lot of bright colours. Our red drawing-room is too bright for some of our friends and visitors.

Above *The Library with its Gothick style windows*
Below *The enormous doll's house is used as a toy cupboard*
Opposite, top left *The Regency barrel organ in the Gothick Room*
Top right *The yellow bedroom: blue and white china of every description decorates the walls. The theme is echoed in the bed-hangings*
Centre left *White and green provide a splendid foil for the vivid red walls in the drawing-room*
Centre right *The windows in the Gothick Room have heavy glazing bars*
Below left *A collection of shells in one of the bedrooms*
Below right *The orange staircase walls were copied from Malahide Castle*

Top row *Viewed from left to right, the front entrance hall and a window in the red drawing-room*
Bottom row *The bed in the main bedroom is domed in the Egyptian style (1835), the stove and carpet are French. The passage on the right is decorated with French wallpaper*
Right *The Library colour scheme is blue, white and gold. The books, with fine gilded bindings, were picked up at local auctions. The chandelier is Italian and the urn on the mantelpiece is a Waterford glass honey jar*

"Don't care for tomato walls meself", I overheard a stranger say when a local charity was temporarily in possession.'

'Do you know anything of any of the people who lived in the Castle before you came here?'

'In common with any other house in Ireland, Leixlip's had its share of eccentric inhabitants. Lord Townshend, the Viceroy, used Leixlip as an occasional summer residence during his five-year term of office from seventeen-sixty-seven. He used to throw open the grounds on Sundays and mingle *incognito* with the visitors who had driven out from Dublin to admire the Salmon Leap and take the waters at Lucan Spa. His visitors would often criticize government policy, never dreaming that they were speaking to the Viceroy himself. Legend has it that one day a poor journeyman-cutler, named Edward Bentley, offered Lord Townshend half-a-crown for his pains in showing all the beauties of the demesne, and was astonished when his tip was refused. "The fellow at the gate-lodge demanded half-a-crown before he would let me in at all", he said. Lord Townshend showed his new friend out. At the lodge he accused the keeper of disobeying his orders by accepting money. The unfortunate man dropped to his knees and begged forgiveness, at which the journeyman-cutler did likewise. Lord Townshend drew his sword and lay it on his friend's shoulder, saying "Arise, Sir Edward Bentley". The newly made Knight was forthwith appointed Cutler to His Excellency!'

INVERARAY CASTLE

THE PRESENT Inveraray Castle was built on almost the same site as the earlier castle built by the Campbells in the first half of the fifteenth century. The old castle was demolished in a grandiose and typical piece of eighteenth-century town-planning.

The present Castle was started by the 3rd Duke of Argyll soon after he succeeded to the title in 1743. He commissioned Roger Morris (1695-1749), who was then 'Carpenter and Principal Engineer to the Board of Ordnance' of which the Duke had been Master-General some years before. Although Morris was better known as a Palladian, he seems to have had no qualms about engaging in gothic for the castle and his plans are preserved at Inveraray.

Morris was not only engaged to design the new Castle; he was also instructed to plan a new town on fairly impressive lines. Unfortunately, Morris died in 1749 and the Duke in 1761, by which time the project was still far from completed: the carcase of the Castle was virtually complete but the project for the new town had been barely started, despite the fact that the work was being supervised by William Adam, a builder and designer of considerable vigour and enterprise, who was succeeded as supervisor of the town building by his son, John Adam, brother of the redoubtable Robert. Understandably, the Castle came first in the Duke's list of priorities.

The 4th Duke rarely visited Inveraray, but the 5th Duke, who succeeded to the title in 1770, set about the completion of the task. To that end he engaged Robert Mylne (1734-1811) to complete the interior of the castle and the town.

Mylne, who was descended from a well-established family of Scottish masons, and was the son of the Surveyor to the City of Edinburgh, ably succeeded in both these tasks. Between 1772 and 1782 he was responsible for the refitting and decoration of the hall, saloon, drawing-room and dining-room and for the completion of the town, his plan based on a central feature, the handsome church in the centre of the town designed by himself.

The Castle is built of blue-grey chlorite slag, quarried at Creggans on nearby Loch Fyne. Although Morris had given the Castle its distinctive and romantic gothic features, Mylne saw no reason to change this theme, although he did reorientate the entrance from the south-west to the north-east, infiltrating three rooms—hall, dining-room and drawing-room—into the resulting space which Morris had intended for a Long Gallery.

The magnificence of the interior of Inveraray is due almost solely to Mylne, although John Adam, following his father, had provided a worthy interior framework in which Mylne was able to exercise his remarkable skills as a decorator, aided by Biagio Rebecca, (1735-1808) the Italian painter.

Opposite *Inveraray Castle and the River Aray, seen from the south*

The 'Circular Room,' in the north turret, houses a collection of porcelain
Opposite *The Duke of Argyll at work in the Brown Library*

THE DUKE OF ARGYLL is a tall, fresh-faced man, direct, quick, articulate. Used to a fairly rigorous physical life, he was chaffing at a temporary immobility imposed by torn ligaments, the result of taking a staircase at Inveraray at too strenuous a tempo. He was taking his enforced inactivity with ill-concealed hostility. 'The doctor tells me I'll be all right in five or six weeks. I hope to God he's right. This kind of thing is intolerable. I have to go to London for treatment next week. That'll be no picnic. Inveraray is no place for a semi-cripple.'

'Perhaps, now that you have decided to leave Inveraray to live abroad, you'd rather not talk about the place.'

'Not at all. One never minds talking about experiences which have given one great pleasure, and certainly Inveraray has given me that. Immense pleasure. No, I'd like to talk about Inveraray. Carry on.'

'When did you inherit Inveraray?'

'In nineteen-forty-nine. From my cousin.'

'Had you always known you'd inherit?'

'More or less.'

'Did you grow up here?'

'No, I was at school in the United States during the First War. I came back and went up to Oxford. After that I went into Fleet Street for a time—my first wife was the daughter of Lord Beaverbrook so I did a stint on the *Evening Standard*. Then I travelled a good deal, and then during the last war I was a prisoner in Germany.'

'Did you find the prospect of inheriting Inveraray at all intimidating?'

'Not really. I'd spent a lot of time here as a boy, and again as a young man. I was on good terms with my cousin. I knew my way around. I'd shot and walked all over the estate. No, it seemed a natural kind of thing. But I was pretty intimidated when I saw what faced me as far as the house was concerned. My cousin had rather let the place go and the amount of work facing me—and the cost—was fairly alarming. For instance, I got a tender at the time for putting in central heating for what you might call the living quarters of the castle. Sixteen thousand pounds for that alone. I suppose it would cost forty thousand today.'

'Did you put it in?'

'Not a chance. There were far too many other things to be done to get things going and to make ends meet. Actually, I use electricity for our private rooms and keep log fires going in the Great Hall throughout the winter. It seems to work quite well, even in the Scottish climate.'

'How much time do you spend at Inveraray?'

'About ten months a year. My London friends often ask me what I find to do up here, but the fact is I never seem to have enough time. You may not know—why should you?—but the archives at Inveraray are probably as voluminous as those of any other large house in Britain. We have records of Clan Campbell going back to the fourteenth century. In fact, the greater part of the history of western Scotland is recorded in the papers here. It would take me another three generations merely to get them in order. I've only recently finished building a new muniments room, but that's scarcely taken care of more than a third of the material—all in steel cases on steel shelving.'

'Do you ever work on the records yourself?'

'Indeed I do. I try to arrange to spend part of every day going through the records. Mostly, I work in the Brown Library during the mornings. In the afternoons I'm usually out of doors.'

The town and castle of Inveraray, separated by nearly half-a-mile, are seen here from across Loch Fyne

'Do you specialize on any particular phase in Scottish history?'

'My studies are partly controlled by the fact that although I can transcribe calligraphy of the late seventeenth century and onwards, I'm not so hot at hands before that time. Those I have to send off to experts at Edinburgh. In any case, being very interested in the estate I'm particularly absorbed in studying the career of the fifth Duke, a soldier who couldn't spend over-much time here, but managed, nevertheless, to carry out some remarkable practical experiments. He tried to educate the local farmers, for instance, into more modern methods—and that at the end of the eighteenth century. He spent enormous sums on demonstrating his ideas and ideals. He was up against some fairly backward types, mind you. The land up here was still being worked by the wooden-bladed plough. He must have been a remarkably energetic man. After ending his army career as a general he then commissioned Robert Mylne to set about replanning and, where necessary, rebuilding the town along lines already laid down by John Adam.'

'The town had been removed and rebuilt some time before, hadn't it?'

'Yes, one of my predecessors, the third Duke, not only commissioned Roger Morris to build a new castle, but also to build a new town on Gallows Foreland where it still stands. That was in the seventeen-forties. I suppose it was one of the earliest examples of town-planning on a rational basis. The town still seems to give architects a good deal of visual pleasure when they come up here.'

'Presumably you also have a fair number of historians as visitors?'

'Quite a lot seem to find the archives here extremely useful when working for their doctorates. I suppose in the years to come there'll be hundreds of hopeful young historians coming over from American universities to do research—once all the classification's finished. At the present rate that'll be in about forty years' time.'

'Do you find the Castle fairly easy to live in?'

'Very. In fact, as you can see, it's fairly small by great house standards. But I've had to work hard to make it this way. When I came here in 'forty-nine there was one bathroom awaiting me, with one more for the staff in the basement. We've put in a few more since then, I'm happy to say.'

'Is keeping up the Castle much of a problem?'

'Running the place has its headaches. My cousin had eleven maids, for instance, as well as butler, footmen, kitchen staff, four gardeners and so on. I have a cook and a maid. I had a gardener. Then I didn't have a gardener. Now I've got a gardener. It goes like that. One doesn't know what the future holds for those who come after.'

'One gardener seems fairly short-staffed for a garden this size.'

'One just can't get 'em.'

'How large is the garden?'

'Twenty-six acres immediately surrounding the house. But it's not just the gardening. It's the incalculables. In the gales last year we lost over ninety-thousand cubic feet of timber. Trees down all over the place. We haven't cleared them all yet. Yet one wants to keep the place up to standard with the Castle open from Easter onwards.'

'When did you first open the Castle to the public?'

'In nineteen-fifty-three.'

'Did you mind?'

'Not a bit. I knew it was the only way to keep the house going. It was that or leaving the roof off and letting the whole place go to pot, and I wasn't prepared to do that.'

'How many visitors do you get?'

'About seventy thousand a year between Easter Saturday and mid-October. But the Castle isn't exactly made for the easy circulation of, say, a thousand people a day. It isn't one of those enormous shapeless castles; in fact, it's rather compact. But we do our best and most visitors

seem to enjoy themselves.'

'Seventy thousand seems a sizable total for Argyllshire. It's scarcely the Home Counties.'

'It's not bad, but it's not nearly enough to make it a profitable venture. It helps to keep the place maintained. I imagine one needs the numbers they get at Longleat or Woburn to get into the real money. I suppose Montagu at Beaulieu does best, but he's got all those cars and Longleat has all those lions. We've no gimmicks of any kind here, I'm thankful to say.'

'But you'd like a lot more visitors?'

'I would indeed, but considering how far north we are and the state of the hotel industry in Scotland and the road system, we do quite well. Scotland, unfortunately, still isn't equipped for tourism judged by continental standards, although I always think that the tourist potential in Scotland is enormous. But currently we're not offering the tourists what they want. "Americans want tea at one in the afternoon," I'm told by the hoteliers. "What shall we do?" "Give it to 'em," I say. "We need to counteract some of the drawbacks of our climate by the warmth of our welcome."'

Above *The Garron Lodge, about a mile from the castle*
Opposite above *The Duke and Duchess's private drawing-room*
Below, right *The Victorian Bedroom contains many relics of Queen Victoria and her daughter Princess Louise*
Left *An imposing four-poster in a round, turret bedroom*

'How do you enjoy the Scottish weather yourself?'

'I like it. One gradually becomes waterproofed. But this past year, of course, we've had quite fantastic weather. I haven't known a summer like it since 'thirty-five. If we could have that every year, tourism in Scotland would be a very different matter indeed.'

'How large are the Inveraray estates?'

'About forty thousand acres. We go down into Kintyre—that's the tip of Scotland that almost touches Ireland—and we have land in the southern part of Mull.'

'Do you farm?'

'We have ten farms in hand. But farming in Scotland is a dicey business. We simply haven't enough lowland. I think the future must inevitably rest with forestry. We can plant up to eight hundred feet and the Forestry Commission can plant from eight hundred feet upwards. In my own case we work closely with the Forestry Commission so that we can share fencing costs and things like that. A private forester simply can't pay wages to compete with the Forestry Commission. And that, I'm afraid, goes for the rest of the Highlands. Young people simply have to leave to get any kind of money at all: they either go and work on the conveyor-

belts in Glasgow or go abroad. I suppose sooner rather than later the stretch between Glasgow and Edinburgh will be one great factory belt. I'm afraid that Scotsmen are at their best when they emigrate, which may be another way of saying the most enterprising do emigrate. The trouble is that those left behind are the older and least adventurous people. It's one of Scotland's major problems.'

'As head of Clan Campbell, do you get many Campbell visitors?'

'From all over the world. Four or five thousand of them annually. They all sign the visitors' book, but whether they're all Campbells is another matter. If I were to take that as any guide, the Campbells would half-cover the world.'

'Does your wife like Inveraray?'

'Adores it. Fortunately, she's also interested in the records here and has her own lines of inquiry.'

'And your sons?'

'My elder son loves the place, and as he also has a son it all helps to give a sense of continuity to the place.'

'You say you spend most afternoons on the estate. Is that mainly concerned with the running of the estate or your sporting life?'

'Almost exclusively on affairs of the estate. The farms, cottages, fencing, planting and felling, and the hundred-and-one things inseparable from a place like this. As for the sporting life, I'm afraid that's not what it was. Before the First War, with seven keepers, Inveraray occasionally

Two views of the Tapestry Drawing-Room with a painted and modelled ceiling by Robert Mylne. The Beauvais tapestries date from about 1770. The gilt chairs are covered with Aubusson tapestry. The crystal chandeliers are early nineteenth century

Opposite *The Adam Dining-Room was enhanced by the decoration of Robert Mylne and Biagio Rebecca in 1783. The silver gilted wheeled* nefs *on the table are of German manufacture*
Above *The Armoury Hall and Gallery with the remarkable collection of arms. Some of the examples date from the fifteenth century*

yielded up to two thousand brace of grouse. Now we would be very lucky to get two hundred brace. The Forestry Commission has brought new life to parts of the Highlands but it doesn't seem to have encouraged wild life. One would have thought otherwise.'

'Do you have much to do with the town?'

'That's almost inevitable. I spend a fair amount of time with the town officials. Fortunately, Inveraray as a tourist attraction has brought a good deal of trade to the town. Tea shops and tweed shops have all benefitted. One is glad to see that, but it's not the same as having a healthy economic life running right through the Highlands, which I want to see. Unless we have some kind of economic miracle, I'm afraid we shall only see the area north of here in steady decline.'

'And now you are about to hand over everything to your son.'

'I am, and I can only hope he gets as much pleasure from the place as I have myself.'

WILTON HOUSE

THE EARLY history of Wilton, the supreme example of Caroline architecture, which has been called the most beautiful house in England, remains somewhat confused, despite the researches of architectural historians. The attributions are shared between three men: Isaac de Caus (son of a French architect and himself better known as a garden designer), Inigo Jones, the King's architect, and John Webb, who entered the story at a later stage as supervisor of Jones's final suggestions, the great man then being very old and unable to travel to Wilton.

The basis of the house we see today was established by the 4th Earl of Pembroke, a remarkably successful man of affairs, who combined a passion for high office—and its attendant profits—with a passion for building. Having inherited, in 1630, the Tudor house at Wilton from his elder brother, he set about rebuilding the house. The earliest design, which for many years was attributed to Inigo Jones, is now more acceptably considered to have been basically the work of de Caus, although many of the proposed improvements certainly derived from suggestions made by Jones. Indeed, legend says that the 3rd Earl had sponsored Jones's journey to Italy. As Lord Chamberlain to Charles I, the 4th Earl would have been close to Inigo Jones, architect of the Banqueting House in Whitehall.

In either 1647 or 1648, a disastrous fire occured at Wilton. The South Front, which incorporated the de Caus-Jones work, was destroyed or badly damaged. The earl, undaunted, began to rebuild almost immediately. According to John Aubrey, the house was 're-edifyed' by Jones, then an old man, who seems to have conveyed his ideas to Pembroke by way of John Webb, who probably supervised the ensuing reconstruction and redecorations. The four Italianate towers, which are such an unusual and distinctive feature of Wilton, would certainly seem to have been adaptations suggested by Jones, as were the proposals for the decoration of the great series of State Rooms, the most famous of which are the Double Cube Room (its decorative scheme designed to incorporate the great series of Van Dyck Pembroke family portraits) and the Cube Room. Although the Colonnade Room and Corner Room and Little Ante-Room are much smaller, they share the magnificent decorative qualities of the larger rooms. (The Hunting Room, with its intriguing series of paintings of hunting-scenes by Edward Pierce is possibly pre-fire.)

Some of the original decoration of these rooms was modified in the eighteenth century when the gilt furniture designed by William Kent (and now so appropriate a feature of the room) was introduced.

Wilton has been fortunate in its owners. At the beginning of the eighteenth century the 8th Earl started that programme of redesigning the gardens in the naturalistic manner to supersede the formal gardens established by de Caus. This passion for landscape gardening was continued by his successors well into the nineteenth century. The 9th Earl, who also had a passion for building, and was an architect, built, most notably, with Roger Morris, the enchanting Palladian Bridge, one of the glories of Wilton. At the beginning of the nineteenth century James Wyatt added the cloisters, rebuilt the West Front, designed the North Forecourt and made the sweeping suggestions for the gardens, which remain.

Opposite, top row (*left to right*) *James Wyatt's screen and Sir William Chambers's arch in the Forecourt entrance; detail of arch; Forecourt gates*
Second row *East Front; the 'Holbein' porch; south-east view*
Third row *Statuary group in Forecourt; the Palladian Bridge; the colonnaded interior of the Palladian Bridge*
Bottom row *The famous South Front; the Orangery; lead figures of children in the Italian garden*

SIDNEY CHARLES HERBERT, 16th Earl of Pembroke, 13th Earl of Montgomery, Baron Herbert of Caerdiff, Baron Herbert of Shurland, Baron Herbert of Lea, spends some days of his week in the 400 acres of the park and gardens that comprise the immediate environs of Wilton House, as well as on the farms and woodlands which comprise the Pembroke Estate. When not carrying out public duties, or, for relaxation, fishing and shooting, he is a complete countryman, as well as overseer of the considerable enterprise with which we are here more immediately concerned: How to run a Stately Home in the twentieth century and like it.

[The interview with the 16th Earl of Pembroke, recorded below without amendment, took place at Wilton House a few months before the death of the Earl, in March 1969. It is retained here as the Earl loved Wilton as passionately—and as knowledgeably—as any of his forebears.]

His deep affection for the beautiful and remarkable house which he owns is early evident. He knows every nook and corner of the house, every picture in a prodigious private collection; above all, the lives of his ancestors as if they were his living brothers. He will refer conversationally to the 'Architect Earl', 'The Horsey Earl' and 'Sidney', as if the 9th and 10th Earls and Sidney Herbert (or, more formally, Lord Herbert of Lea), friend of Florence Nightingale, were still around and likely to drop in for a drink later in the day. A visitor, curious about The Architect Earl, will be marched off and shown, first, a portrait of a handsome and intelligent-looking youth and, then, Roubillac's bust of the pugnacious, impregnable man the youth became. Pictures of the profligate 10th Earl abound, for he was a notable horseman with a penchant for having himself painted at the slightest excuse. And the Wilton muniment room, as Lord Pembroke points out, was frequently consulted by Cecil Woodham-Smith for her book on Florence Nightingale. Few aristocrats can be on such pleasant terms with their forebears.

The 16th Earl of Pembroke

This close knowledge derives in part from his own considerable researches, during the past thirty years, into the provenance of the paintings at Wilton, studies which have resulted in a recent publication by the Phaidon Press of *A catalogue of the Paintings and Drawings in the Collection at Wilton House*, a monograph that many a Courtauld Institute graduate would be glad to have linked with his name.

Lord Pembroke came into the title on the death of his father in 1960. He was then in his mid-fifties and had owned Wilton, and been in charge of the estate, for some years before that. Having known and loved the place all his life, he had, unlike many inheritors of historic houses and sizable estates, few qualms about taking on the management and direction of so complex a set-up. Here he had spent a relaxed and happy childhood, holidays from school and university. He appreciated to the full its qualities as a house of unusual history and beauty.

Was he ever intimidated in any degree by the responsibilities of such a house?

'Not really. It's a bit of a problem running a place like this in these days. One wants to do one's best by the house whilst recognizing one is living in a vastly different world from that of one's parents. But one copes.'

'D'you mind seeing hordes of people wandering around the house and gardens during the tourist season?'

'Only for a week or so, perhaps, after we open in April. It's apt to come as a bit of a shock after the long winter when we've been here on our own. During the winter there's a hundred-and-one things to be done, of course, and I suppose we get rather absorbed getting bits and pieces of the house refurnished against the opening—settees re-covered, windows repaired, a cornice repainted and so on. The sudden crowds are, momentarily, a trifle alarming. But the mood soon wears off.'

'Presumably, you've come to accept them by May?'

'Oh, long before that. After all, Wilton was open to the outside world a good deal earlier than any other large house. We had regular visitors from the town coming here as early as the 1850s. And Wilton's always been very closely associated with the town, which was once upon a time capital of Wessex, by the way. And for years the family was involved with the carpet factory in the town, although we're not now. These things help to build up a relationship. We've never been allowed to grow remote and anti-social. The town wouldn't let us.'

'And you don't object?'

'Not a bit. I rather like it. Indeed, one sometimes feels that the town rather regards the house partly as its own. And that kind of feeling can be useful these days, of course. We are very lucky in being able to get help locally. Heaven knows how some of these remoter mansions and castles get by.'

'Did your ancestors see things the same way? After all, those were rather less egalitarian days.'

'Not a bit. They got the thing going. I think this physical proximity to the town is a very real thing. Up till nineteen-twenty, in fact, we had for years had our own school here, in the old seventeenth-century grotto which de Caus designed. The school was for the daughters of the estate staff. In fact, the one-time grotto is now known as the Park School House. There's a picture in my great-grandmother's family album here which shows a group of the pupils. Very pretty uniforms the girls had, too. You couldn't have found a better turned-out group of school children in the whole of England. But that kind of private education ended in nineteen-twenty and the building languished for a time. Then my brother turned it into a quite enchanting house.'

'In the history of some great houses one finds the occasional renegade owner who lets the whole place go to rack and ruin. Did you have any like that?—or have all your ancestors loved the house?'

'In the main I think they all have. After all, it's a very easy house to like. Even Henry, the 10th Earl, who spent a lot of his time travelling on the Continent chasing women, loved Wilton, although he left his wife temporarily (with whom even the waspish Horace Walpole couldn't find fault) after only two years of marriage. I think most of us realize quite early on in our lives that we've something pretty unusual on our hands.'

'If H G Wells' time-machine were available, which of your ancestors would you most like to meet for a conversational interlude?'

'I think Henry in his earlier years must have been rather fun, rake that he was. King George the Third, despite his fondness for Henry's wife, seems to have succumbed to the reprobate's charms. Yes, I think the young Henry would be quite entertaining. And I should like to meet the Architect Earl, formidable as he certainly was. One's only got to look at that extraordinary jaw in the Roubillac bust to see that. And, of course, Thomas, the 8th Earl, who was a great collector, and restored the family fortunes after the death of his dissolute brother, the 7th Earl.'

'What do you regard as your own major contribution to Wilton?'

'Well, running the place and making a go of it in this day and age, I suppose.'

'Does that include running the estate?'

'Everything, from getting leaflets printed for the tourists, to looking after the estate, from organizing guides to running the sawmill.'

'Do all these activities make money?'

'Good heavens, no. Despite some government grants Wilton costs quite a packet to run. One wants the best, I suppose. The woodlands

lose money mainly because I don't run them entirely in the same way the Forestry Commission or a commercial sawmill outfit might run them. I can't take these great plantations of boring softwoods, although they're undeniably more profitable. Like any other countryman, I believe in mixed woodlands—I think they're more logical for England in the long run—but it does mean a sizable investment in slower-growing hardwoods. I suppose my grandchildren will reap some benefit. I certainly won't.'

'Your cedars here are world-famous. Do you still plant them?'

'To celebrate family anniversaries—births, marriages, that sort of thing. All the cedars, incidentally, derive from the original seventeenth-century trees, two of which still survive. Our biggest has a girth, by the way, of well over thirty feet.'

'Have you done anything to the house which gives you particular pleasure?'

'Apart from painting the Upper Cloisters terracotta and grey, replacing Wyatt's heavy gothic cupola, by one more in keeping with the Tudor tower on which it rests, gave me as much pleasure as anything I've done. I evolved a design with our then-Clerk of the Works, Mr Austen, an

Above, left *The East side of the Upper Cloisters, added by James Wyatt in the early nineteenth century*
Right *The statue of Shakespeare in the Hall was designed by William Kent in 1747*

unusual man who'd trained as an architect and was a superb draughtsman. It's the one you see now—mainly built of teak and lead-covered. The teak's weathered extremely well. We managed to incorporate the old clock, too. Made in Windsor in seventeen forty-five and still going strong. Most architects seem to agree that we did rather well.'

'Which part of the house gives you greatest pleasure?'

'Well, obviously the Double Cube Room, which is a most marvellous room. One studies the room year after year and still keeps discovering new charms, despite some very curious oddities of proportion which outwit any explanation the experts can think up.'

'What kind of oddities?'

'Well, the room was obviously planned as a perfect Double Cube Room —sixty by thirty by thirty—but the kind of symmetry such a room demands just isn't there. The windows aren't symmetrically placed; the great Venetian window and the fireplace aren't dead opposite the centre of the painted ceiling, and certain motifs in the painting of the covered ceiling are way out: quite fascinating.'

'What other rooms please you?'

'All the sixteenth- and seventeenth-century rooms in the South and East sides of the house.'

'Wilton isn't too demanding a Stately Home, then?'

'As a house I find Wilton an easy place to live in. There's nothing intimidating about any part of it. Even the Double Cube Room isn't a bit overpowering. Neither is the Single Cube Room. And none of the bedrooms in the upper part of the house is a stately stateroom or anything like that. Even the so-called Colonnade Room, our nearest approach to a King's Bedroom—Queen Charlotte slept there—is quite manageable.'

'And which of Wilton's façades gives you most pleasure?'

'The South Front, of course. Everything about that seems perfect: the proportions, the Venetian window centrepiece, the windows, the towers, everything. I always thank my lucky stars that we were spared Isaac de Caus's suggested South Front. Wilton would have been more like a block of government offices if that had been accepted.'

'But you wouldn't call de Caus a bad architect.'

'On the contrary. It was just that his suggestions for the South Front were rather over-serious. The old stables he designed up on the hill must be amongst the most enchanting buildings in England. The Ministry of Works seems to think them well worth preserving and so do all the architectural historians. And half my friends want to convert them into a weekend folly. It wouldn't work, but I see their point.'

'Judging by the scaffolding, the Palladian Bridge seems to be undergoing repairs. Are they serious?'

'Fairly, but not very, is probably the answer. Apparently most of the iron cramps Roger Morris put into his stonework, presumably to strengthen it, had rusted up and weakened the stonework. It was, after all, built between seventeen thirty-five and seventeen thirty-seven. Fortunately, the stonemasons seem to be doing a fine renovating job, tricky as it is.'

'Insurance must be a terrifying problem here.'

'Well it is and it isn't. The basic and inescapable fact is that the worth of a place like this is incalculable. How does one value a house that could never be rebuilt? How could we begin to replace the pictures? Or the furniture? We have a global arrangement with the insurers with no single object liable for more than a certain sum. It could be a nightmare, of course, but one learns to live with it. I sleep very well because we have a night watchman, and police very close.'

'Does the annual invasion take away *all* your privacy?'

'We manage to preserve a reasonable piece of the place to ourselves. We rope off this Western side of the house and that gives us a pleasantly unspoiled outlook over the formal garden from the Library and the Dining-Room. It also includes our own pool and the Orangery. So we can't grumble.'

'And nobody invades?'

'The occasional interloper who climbs over or under the rope and then says he or she's lost the way, even though they're standing there with a cine-camera going full blast documenting me in the swimming-pool. Human nature being what it is, I suppose anything sealed off has its own special allure.'

'You seem free from the kind of sideshows which other Stately Homes—let them be nameless—seem to find necessary to add to their attractions. Is this so?'

'Basically, yes, although we are singularly—quite literally—rich in one curious sideshow. That's a collection of toy soldiers, seven thousand of them, which I inherited from one of my uncles. Beautiful things. German-

Opposite *The Single Cube Room. Above the fireplace is a portrait of Henriette de Kerouaille, wife of the 7th Earl, by Sir Peter Lely*

made in about nineteen hundred. It's a unique collection, I believe, and I had an entertaining and instructive time arranging them in some kind of battle order. Young boys seem to find it a pleasant relief from architecturally-minded mamas and the house and gardens. We took over a hundred-and-fifty pounds last year and the year before—at sixpence a time. Not bad. They're in a small room off the old riding-school.'

'Do you spend most of your life here?'

'I can scarcely bear to be away. It's pleasant to go abroad or to visit one's friends and we go to London fairly frequently, but one always wants to get back here as soon as possible. My wife feels the same way.'

The Pembrokes live in what was the Library, and is now a handsome

Left *The fireplace in the Corner Room with a portrait of Prince Rupert of the Rhine above*
Opposite *The Double Cube Room, built in the mid seventeenth century, measures sixty feet long, by thirty, by thirty. The ceiling surrounds are the work of Edward Pierce*

Opposite *The Hunting Room with panels showing hunting-scenes by Edward Pierce*
Above *The Smoking Room, showing the Chippendale bookcase and some of the Spanish 'Haute Ecole' gouache drawings*

sitting-room, over sixty-feet long, papered in a mellow Coles honey-gold and grey wallpaper with a six-foot repeat motif. The room, overlooking the formal garden with a vista terminated by the 'Holbein' porch, glows in the afternoon sun. They have also converted the one-time Breakfast Room on the ground floor into a charming low-ceilinged private dining-room. This room spent part of its earlier life, in the eighteenth century, as a Pompeian Bath with sunken heated bath and Corinthian columns to boot. The Russian Lady Pembroke, born Catherine Woronzow, swept away the bath in about 1815, to make the Breakfast Room. Now the room is papered with a Chinese wallpaper on a rich blue background. Only shreds of old paper remained in nineteen sixty but samples were sent to Hong-Kong and the paper was hand-copied at modest expense by Chinese craftsmen who recognized the design as an eighteenth-century paper once made specially for the English market. With its southern and western outlook over the vast lawns, the Chinese wallpaper and simulated bamboo gothick surrounds to glazed china cabinets, the room is pleasantly dichotomous in mood, rather like an Oriental tea-room set in an English landscape garden.

Few owners of Stately Homes have managed so skilfully to infiltrate a comfortable and relaxed twentieth-century life into so palatial a relic from another age as the Pembrokes at Wilton.

CASTLE HOWARD

'AS A FIRST essay in architecture, Castle Howard in Yorkshire has never been really credible', wrote Laurence Whistler in 1954, in what remains the most exhaustive and exciting of all accounts of Vanbrugh and his works.* He then goes on to show that although there is no reason to doubt that the great house which we see today was basically Vanbrugh's, the technical working out of the plan undoubtedly owed a very great deal to Nicholas Hawksmoor.

The story is both hazy and complex, and, unfortunately, the original source material is either lost or still too limited for the authentic story ever likely to be unravelled. Yet the house that the two architects built, ably supported by their patron, Lord Carlisle, now ranks amongst the great houses of Europe. That is certain.

Castle Howard succeeded an older house known as Henderskelfe Castle, largely rebuilt in 1683 and burnt out ten years later, about which curiously little is known. It also supplants the old church, village and gardens as well, for they all had to make way for the new house.

After the new house was projected, plans were first prepared by William Talman, then Comptroller of the Works. Partly due to his own self-esteem and partly to Vanbrugh's friendship with Carlisle, he was ousted from both the Comptrollership and the Castle Howard project.

Yet none of the manoeuvres and intrigues which attended the early proposals for the house explains the supreme assurance and sophistication with which Vanbrugh moved in. He was not only able to design a great house but was also persuasive enough to convince the worldly Carlisle, then thirty, that these sketches by an amateur architect embodied all that his lordship was looking for in the great house he wished to build. The story remains one of the most tantalizing mysteries of our architectural history.

Fortunately, however, we do know, and see, the result. Although nothing that can authoritatively be labelled as the original plan survives, certain early sketches are in existence (at the Victoria and Albert Museum). They show tentative essays, each moving more closely towards the house we see today. Obviously much was changed in the course of building, as was usual at the time.

Unfortunately, the building as intended by Carlisle and Vanbrugh, started in 1700, was never completed. Instead, between 1753 and 1759 Sir William Robinson, Carlisle's son-in-law, added the vast new West Wing with its immensely long Long Gallery. But this was years after the death, in 1724, of Vanbrugh (for whom and for whose work Robinson had little or no regard). The addition seriously diminished the unity and vitality of the Vanbrugh-Hawksmoor designs, but certainly did not destroy the essential concept—as any visitor can see.

Perhaps Vanbrugh's own words best sum up the Castle Howard project: 'There being many more Valluable and Agreeable things and Places to be Seen, than in the Tame Sneaking South of England.'

Opposite *The north façade with the Vanbrugh entrance, East Wing and Robinson West Wing*

**The Imagination of Vanbrugh and his Fellow Artists:* by Laurence Whistler. (Art & Technics and Batsford)

EIGHT MILES out of York, moving swiftly on the uncrowded A64 to Malton and Scarborough, the signpost to CASTLE HOWARD can easily be overshot, for it is a curiously reticent and modest guide to one of the most spectacular houses in Europe.

The modesty doesn't, however, persist for very long. The house, seen far off, is an astonishing building to find astride the first hills to halt the wide north-west vistas of the Plain of York. The gilded lantern of the great dome of the palatial house catches the morning sun.

The road to the house soon becomes a five-mile essay in eighteenth-century arrogance or, at least, self-confidence, for it runs, as straight as a rule, to the house. Two centuries ago the prospect must have seemed even more assured, for then the beech trees were growing towards maturity, but even today, nearer the house, the double row of limes—among the oldest in the country—still makes a superb approach during the summer months.

But nature was never enough for Charles Howard, 3rd Earl of Carlisle. He wanted an approach to his house commensurate with its own grandeur. In addition to the avenues he demanded memorials and objects that would evoke the proper mood in a visitor. Awe mingled with respect, perhaps. Nothing simple or normal. That was certain. So he built the Carrmire Gate and its battlements across the road. Then, half-a-mile further on, Vanbrugh's machiolated arch with its assertive pyramid.

Above *George and Lady Cecilia Howard and their four sons*
Below *The interior of the great dome of Castle Howard, now spectacularly restored, after its destruction by fire in* 1940
Opposite *The Mausoleum, designed by Hawksmoor*

The south approach to Castle Howard

Then, at the intersection of the north-south, east-west avenues leading to the house, the hundred-foot stone obelisk, which prefaces its inscriptional record of the Earl's building and planting activities with these lines:

If to perfection these plantations rise
If they agreeably my heirs surprise
This faithful pillar will their age declare
As long as time these characters shall spare
Here then with kind remembrance read his name
Who for posterity performed the same

Then on to the house, passing, on the right, the stables, a splendid and serene honey-toned stone block built round a quadrangle by John Carr of York, between 1781 and 1784.

The house, of course, is fantastic, fabulous, incredible.

How could any man, the visitor finds himself asking time and again, how could any man in his right senses even contemplate the building of such a palace in the wilds of Yorkshire, three or four days' journeying from London? How could he?—even though he owned the land for miles around, even though he was acting Earl Marshal at the time and destined to be First Lord of the Treasury at a later date?

Well, he did, and there's an end to it, as Vanbrugh probably said, for he was the man who aided and abetted the 3rd Earl in his vast and grandiose monomania. Little wonder that Horace Walpole, after visiting the house, wrote: 'Nobody had informed me that at one view I should

see a palace, a town, a fortified city, temples on high places, woods worthy of being each a metropolis of the Druids, the noblest lawn in the world fenced by half the horizon, and a mausoleum that would tempt one to be buried alive; in short, I have seen gigantic palaces before, but never a sublime one.'

The house, built of tawny stone quarried locally, stands above and within a thousand-acre park, mostly encompassed by a wall. Much of this onetime parkland is now intensively farmed. From the house the outlook is various and wide-ranging; lawns, farmland, woodland, formal gardens.

Millions of film-goers have seen the house, most probably without realizing that they were looking at Castle Howard, which was the setting for major sequences of *Lady L*, a rather overblown film starring Sophia Loren, David Niven and Paul Newman, who were, in turn, easily overblown by the beauty of the house.

The exterior is magnificent, but the magnificence of the façades of this seemingly symmetrical masterpiece (which is, in fact, curiously asymmetrical) is dwarfed by the breath-taking qualities of the Hall.

The visitor who is aware of the rudiments of Castle Howard's history is almost at a disadvantage here. The difficulty of taking in the fact that this grand and complex Hall was one of Vanbrugh's first steps in architecture is well-nigh insurmountable.

The Hall is eighty feet high, rising to the top-most curves of the cupola, and fifty-two feet square. The soaring splendours are free of all architectural pomposity. What has been termed its 'sumptuous gaiety' makes this a domestic interior without parallel in England: it is more like the interior of a cathedral dedicated to the livelier pagan deities of the visual arts than the entry to a house, however grand.

About half the rooms now open to the public are in the West or Robinson Wing, so called because the original Carlisle-Vanbrugh-Hawksmoor conception was drastically modified by the work of Sir Thomas Robinson, an architectural dilettante of considerable assurance and pertinacity, who was son-in-law of the 3rd Earl and brother-in-law of the 4th. He got his chance after the death of Hawksmoor and built on to the incomplete Vanbrugh wing the West Wing with its vast Long Gallery.

Sir Thomas is an outstanding example of the pathological inability of architects to recognize the existence of merit in the work of other architects, however notable. Robinson saw little in the unfinished Vanbrugh masterpiece but a chance to demonstrate his own limited skills. Indeed he would have altered the whole building to conform to his conventional Palladian taste if he'd been given the chance. Fortunately, he wasn't a bad architect. As the present owner says: 'As architecture, it's unobjectionable, but it scarcely harmonizes with Vanbrugh's work.'

The Howards thus lost for ever the chance of getting *in toto* the original Vanbrugh-Hawksmoor elevations, although the Vanbrugh imprint dominates the house. The two present generations of Howards, however, enjoy the next best thing. George and Lady Cecilia Howard and their four sons now live in Vanbrugh's East Wing, and, within this extraordinary house, have infiltrated a warm and comfortable, up-to-date home which faces north, overlooking the lake and park, thus enjoying the ever-changing light on the Yorkshire landscape.

George Howard is forceful and articulate, quick and clear-thinking, his sense and sensibility perhaps superficially belied by his burly and energetic figure.

His energy is formidable. As if running Castle Howard and its ten thousand acres weren't task enough to keep a man busy, his Reliant Scimitar and the M1 keep him in weekly touch with London and a set of extramural chores that would put down most other men for a compulsory count. He is President of the Country Landowners' Association and a member of the Countryside Commission and has recently joined the Council of the Royal College of Art. 'I enjoy these metropolitan contacts,' he says. 'In fact, I don't object to London life the way so many countrymen do. I shoot but don't hunt. I love Castle Howard. I run it as a Stately Home—efficiently, I hope—with the help of my wife and a highly competent comptroller. I farm seventeen hundred acres on my own account—with a manager. But I enjoy my outside interests. I suppose I like what might be called the complications and the manipulations of London.'

'Why?—with Castle Howard so marvellous a place to live and work in?'

'Excess of energy, I suppose. And, of course, a kind of built-in notion that one ought to be up and doing things. One's always chary of using words like duty and responsibilities these days, but something like that would probably fill the bill.'

'But Castle Howard *does* mean a lot to you?'

'But of course. Everything about it. But even that's a kind of public responsibility as well as being one's own home. My father, showing people round, used sometimes to point to something or other somebody had given him and say "That's mine". The rest of it was also his, of course, but there's something of a sense of trusteeship for inherited treasures.'

'Has Castle Howard always had visitors?'

'For as long as I can remember we've had people coming here—over one hundred thousand visitors came last year. But tourists have been visiting Castle Howard ever since it was built. In the early nineteenth century, Colonel Daniel Paterson, who published annual reviews of the roads of England, wrote something to the effect that "the liberality of the noble proprietor in admitting the public to view this elegant repository entitles him to grateful applause". Very civil words, don't you think?'

'And you don't mind it still being that kind of place?'

'Not at all. I sometimes view it as if it belonged to the outside world, which, in a way, I suppose it does—as my father recognized.'

'When did you first realize that it was yours?'

'If at all, rather late and tragically. My father, who was no great believer in primogeniture, left the house equally to my elder brother, Mark; my younger brother, Christopher, and myself. We were all in the war—I was in Burma—and they were both killed in Europe. So it came to me.'

'In good shape?'

'Not particularly. In fact in terrible shape. For one thing we had a dreadful fire here in nineteen-forty, during the war. We had a girls' school here and somehow the fire brigade wasn't called in very early in the proceedings—amongst other mishaps. Part of the South Front was gutted. The cupola and lantern of the dome were destroyed.'

'And you moved in when?'

'We were married in nineteen-forty-nine and moved back here four years later.'

'Undeterred.'

'Unnerved, possibly, but determined.'

'You've now restored the cupola.'

'Yes, but, as you see, the South Front entrance is still pretty rugged and basic, right back to the bare stonework. I don't know whether we'll ever be able to restore that. It would mean building a new house within a house to get it back to what it was. It took some hard work and a great deal of money even to restore it to its present shape, with new windows and roof.'

'Apart from the South Front disaster, would you say it's now pretty much as it's always been?'

'Not quite. We had some rather aged trustees who sold a good deal of the furniture, alas, during the war. They thought we'd never be able to live in the house again. They also sold a lot of fine pictures at the bottom of the market. Those, too, I regret. Who wouldn't regret losing a dozen Canalettos, amongst other things?'

'But it all looks pretty impressive now.'

'I'm glad you think so, but I can tell you that it's pretty hard and continuous work which will probably last the rest of my life. One can spend twenty thousand pounds on the stonework here without anybody but a specialist realizing it.'

'The restoration of the cupola and lantern is, I suppose, the most spectacular of the restorations?'

'The most spectacular of the exterior work. It's all the unseen items that gallop away with the money. A modest area of woodworm or dry rot can really send our budget haywire.'

'What are your first memories of the house?'

'Can't remember. Happily I suffer from total non-recall and am apt to live entirely in the present and the future. When a man says that his schooldays were the happiest of his life I suspect his present existence is very dull indeed. My trouble is trying to crowd a thirty-six-hour day into twenty-four.'

Opposite, top *The gilded lantern of the great dome of Castle Howard*
Centre *Two views of the Temple of the Four Winds*
Below *Decorative visitors' cars designed by Felix Kelly*

'Isn't it pretty overpowering living in a place like Castle Howard?'

'Well, we only live in this one wing and, as you see, it's pretty comfortable. Vanbrugh once wrote that all Lord Carlisle's rooms "with moderate fires are ovens"—and his boast was well-founded. It sounds a preposterous thing to say but when our four sons are home in the holidays, we don't have overmuch room. We have a *pied à terre* in London, but this is our home. And we like it. It's a marvellous house to live in.'

'Your wife has one or two reservations about Vanbrugh as an architect. Do you share them? Too many corridors and so on?'

'That's true. But he was, after all, building a palace, and the plans matched the particular needs of his client. Fortunately, his patron was also a friend.'

'Do you have any records of the Vanbrugh–Lord Carlisle relationship?'

'Some letters. They've all been published in Laurence Whistler's fine book on Vanbrugh.'

'What do *you* think of Vanbrugh after twenty years in the house?'

'Well, he was certainly a strange man to turn architect. Not many architects have been soldiers and dramatists first, have they? I think both talents are given full scope here. Like any good cavalryman Vanbrugh had a sound eye for country and took full advantage of the setting here. And Castle Howard is a dramatist's dream come true. So let's forgive him the corridors.'

'Have you any idea, apart from the correspondence, of how he worked with your ancestor?'

'I imagine that it was mainly by discussion, Vanbrugh, with or without Hawsksmoor, putting up an idea to Lord Carlisle and then the two or three of them kicking it around. My own feeling has always been—and I'm glad to see it's beginning to get some backing from the pundits these days—that Lord Carlisle took a far greater part in the planning and conception of the house than he's so far been given credit for. Carlisle, Vanbrugh and Hawskmoor must have worked together as an unusually amicable team. Certainly Carlisle and Vanbrugh had considerable *rapport*. Undoubtedly they talked the same language. After all, they were both men of the world, both members of the Kit Kat Club.'

'And Hawksmoor?'

'Well, obviously he wasn't part of their social world, but everyone seems to agree that he must have been a man of extraordinarily impressive character and achievement and he certainly took no back seat. The other two needed him for his vast technical knowledge. So I like to think it was a very rare and well-balanced trio who designed this extraordinary place.'

'Do you have any other side-shows?—they seem to be necessary adjuncts of the Stately Homes life.'

'We do have very fine Costume Galleries housed in the stables, but that's all. That's run by Miss Cecile Hummel who's very knowledgeable concerning the history of costume. She started the galleries with her own collection and it's been considerably augmented by gifts and loans. We now have over two thousand costumes in the museum.'

'And it's very popular?'

'Over forty-six thousand people visited the museum last year. The costumes are presented in a series of period settings. The whole project is a serious effort—and schools are beginning to find the galleries highly instructive. So, too, are stage designers.'

'No other side-shows?'

'Well we do take visitors from the house to the galleries in a couple of very decorative cars designed for us by Felix Kelly. I doubt whether any Stately Home has anything as entertaining to put on parade.'

Two views of the Great Hall, which rises 80 feet to the cupola. The chimneypiece is the work of two Italian stuccoists, Bagutti and Plura. The fireplace surround is in scagliola, an imitation marble. The great columns were carved by Samuel Carpenter, a Yorkshire mason

Opposite above *The Tapestry Room in which were formerly hung the tapestries of the Four Seasons. It is now furnished as a dining-room*
Below left *The painted fourposter in the largely unchanged bedroom of Georgiana, wife of the 6th Earl of Carlisle*
Below right *Corridor in the East Wing*
Above *The Gold Library: so called from the Kentian-type pedimented bookcase in white and gilt which dominates one wall. It is now used as a private drawing-room*
Above right *Lady Georgiana's Dressing Room*
Below *A corner of Lady Cecilia Howard's sitting-room in the East Wing*

'No other distractions?'

'Well, yes. Jim Russell, the famous garden designer, has recently moved up here from Sunningdale, bringing his marvellous collection of rhododendrons with him. That will make a difference and an additional pleasure for visitors who happen to be gardeners.'

'Would you describe the Temple of the Four Winds and the Mausoleum as additional pleasures?'

'I think so. The Temple must be one of the half-dozen most enchanting buildings in Britain, don't you think? Just that one extraordinarily beautiful room with a domed ceiling looking out from four sides over the Yorkshire scene. We've had one dinner party there, but the Yorkshire climate isn't conducive to many picnics of that kind, even in high summer.'

'And the Mausoleum?'

'Well, as you'll see, it's a strangely impressive building. Many people think it's Hawksmoor's masterpiece. I find it a supremely satisfying building, and I fully intend to be buried there! And it remains a favourite destination for the more energetic of our visitors. Unfortunately, it's in real danger of collapse. It needs to be a millionaire's solitary hobby. In fact, Castle Howard could take care of the pocket-money of a dozen millionaires.'

But, meantime, George Howard, surveying his domain, seems not unduly perturbed by the manifold problems lurking round the four corners of his vast and splendid heritage. He seems well able to cope.

BLENHEIM PALACE

FOLLOWING his victory at Blenheim over the forces of Louis XIV, the manor of Woodstock in Oxfordshire was bestowed upon the Duke of Marlborough by a then-munificent Queen, representing a grateful nation.

Of any royal instructions concerning the erection of a castle or palace there is no record, although something of this order was probably her intention. Nevertheless, on this somewhat casual basis and a far-from-clear-cut document (whereas the Duke had 'resolved to erect a large Fabrik') from Godolphin, the Royal Treasurer, requested by Vanbrugh, the building was begun. The plan was based upon a scaled up-version of Vanbrugh's first great house, Castle Howard. A model was made for the Queen's approval and the foundation stone was laid on the 18th June, 1705.

Although the Duke and his architect were scarcely acquainted before the Blenheim project, they became friends as the building progressed, and might well have remained so had Sarah, the first Duchess, not interfered. Her vain and domineering personality, however, made clashes inevitable. Yet, despite a thousand difficulties, physical and personal, the gigantic building did, over two decades, slowly progress.

The stone for the building came from quarries in Woodstock Park, but gradually other more distant sources, offering a harder stone, were brought into use; it has been estimated that almost two dozen quarries contributed to the final building. The masons engaged by Vanbrugh were among the foremost in the land, notably Edward Strong and his like-named son, fresh from work on St Paul's.

Not all the innumerable trials and tribulations attending the course of the building were due to the Duchess alone. Vanbrugh frequently changed his mind and his designs, adding a colossal portico and enlarging the Great Hall, both entailing enormous revisions to the initial design. Later still, he changed even the architectural order from Doric to Corinthian—and this despite the fact that the building was already 27 feet high! Throughout the summer of 1707 architect and Duchess vied with each other in pulling down parts of the building and rebuilding to a new design or on a fresh whim. The most depressing fact of all was that cash was always short, and after 1712 contributions from the Lord Treasurer ceased altogether, so that the Marlboroughs were on their own.

By then Marlborough was fighting in Europe once again, with enemies at Court only too anxious to see him in disgrace. Throughout this time the Duchess was quarrelling ceaselessly with Vanbrugh, seeking, in her own words, 'to prevent his extravagance,' but also seeking to supervise the building whilst advising the Duke of progress on the house.

In 1710 the Duchess finally fell out with the Queen (having been superseded in royal favour by Mrs Masham). Difficulties increased on all sides. Work on the house stopped completely in 1712, and in that year Sarah joined her husband abroad.

Building was resumed in 1716 after Queen Anne's death and the Marlboroughs' return from Europe to something approaching their earlier dignity and authority under George I.

In that year, the Duchess ousted Vanbrugh from Blenheim, appointing in his place a cabinet-maker, one John Moore, as her Clerk-of-the-Works and went on with the tremendous task alone. By then the Duke was ailing and well content to leave everything to his formidable wife. The Marlboroughs moved into the eastern wing of the house in 1719 but the Duke had little enough time to spend there. A little over two years later he was dead.

The building of the great palace staggered on, the indefatigable Sarah bringing the house to completion, adding her own salutes to her long-suffering but well-loved husband in Hawksmoor's Triumphal Arch and the Column of Victory. As for Vanbrugh, he caught a glimpse of his masterpiece in 1719, but on a visit in 1725 with his wife was denied entry on the Duchess's express command. He died à year later.

Although he had meantime been occupied with other considerable projects—Eastbury, Seaton Delaval, Grimsthorpe among them—Blenheim was undoubtedly the house he most cherished: in his own words, 'a sort of Child.'

Opposite *The North Front, seen from across the Lake designed by 'Capability' Brown*

AN EMPHASIS on the privacy of Blenheim is quickly made known to the intending visitor.

Entering Woodstock on the A34, he is directed away from the more obvious, but private, Bladon Gate towards another turning on the left. There, by way of an apparent cul-de-sac, he enters beneath the first of the great gates: Hawksmoor's Triumphal Arch, which the townsfolk of Woodstock never wanted, the lodges inserted within the plinths.

Thence into the Park. Here, too, another notice on a grass verge reminds the visitor that Blenheim is a private residence and that the house is open only at certain hours. Proceeding, he passes through the East Gate, Vanbrugh's Cistern Tower (with additions by Sir William Chambers), then through the arch of the clock-tower into the full splendours, architectural and scenic, of Blenheim Palace.

Few, surveying the vast and implacably serene, honey-toned North Front of the house, overlooking the Park, the Grand Bridge and the Lake, could begin to apprehend that its building occasioned more controversy, venom, litigation, sheer pettiness and bloody-mindedness than any other house, great or small, in the history of English architecture.

The story of the vindictive vendetta by Sarah, Duchess of Marlborough, against her architect, Sir John Vanbrugh, is well known. 'Painters, poets and builders have very high flights,' the Duchess observed, 'but they must be kept down.' The trouble was that Sir John was the kind of builder whose genius could not be kept down. The tale of the feud has been told at length by two of Britain's ablest architectural narrators: in the round by David Green*; from the architect's viewpoint by Laurence Whistler**. Anyone who gets caught by the fantastical elements of the Blenheim saga is advised to consult those two books forthwith. Together they will make a worthwhile winter's browsing and study.

The mere statistics of the house are daunting enough: the buildings and courts cover seven acres and the Great Court alone three acres. The North Front is 480 feet long and that of the South 320 feet. The Park, of nearly 2,500 acres, is encompassed by a dry-stone wall about nine miles long, the first built in England, legend says. The Grand Bridge is 390 feet in length, with a central span of over 100 feet.

The interior of the house offers some equally formidable figures. The Great Hall is 70 feet by 45 feet and 67 feet high; the Long Library 183 feet by 22 feet; a typical bedroom 37 feet by 33 feet; the kitchen (now the Audit Room) 50 feet by 28 feet and 32 feet high!

Nobody, certainly not Sarah, ever accused Vanbrugh of cheeseparing, either in his ideas or in seeking to carry them out.

Yet after all the statistics and dimensions of this palace have been noted and absorbed, the visitor begins to make the vain attempt—as in all Vanbrugh's houses—to seek out the kind of man he was. What kind of man could not only evolve buildings of the size and grandeur of Castle Howard, Blenheim, Seaton Delaval, but actually persuade patrons to go along with him, and pay for them? After all, he wasn't building for kings but for private citizens, and although the Queen and Treasury set about underpinning the building of Blenheim the penny-pinching began fairly early on. Basically, he must have been one of nature's spellbinders. We all know that he was a genial wit of unsurpassed self-confidence and equanimity. He must also have been something of a magician with words (after all, he was a successful playwright) and pencil.

The 10th Duke of Marlborough

Opposite *The magnificently-proportioned Great Hall is sixty-seven feet high; the stone decoration and Corinthian columns of the portico were carved by Gibbons*

**Blenheim Palace*, by David Green (Country Life, 1951)

***The Imagination of Vanbrugh and His Fellow Artists*, by Laurence Whistler (Art and Technics with Batsford, 1954)

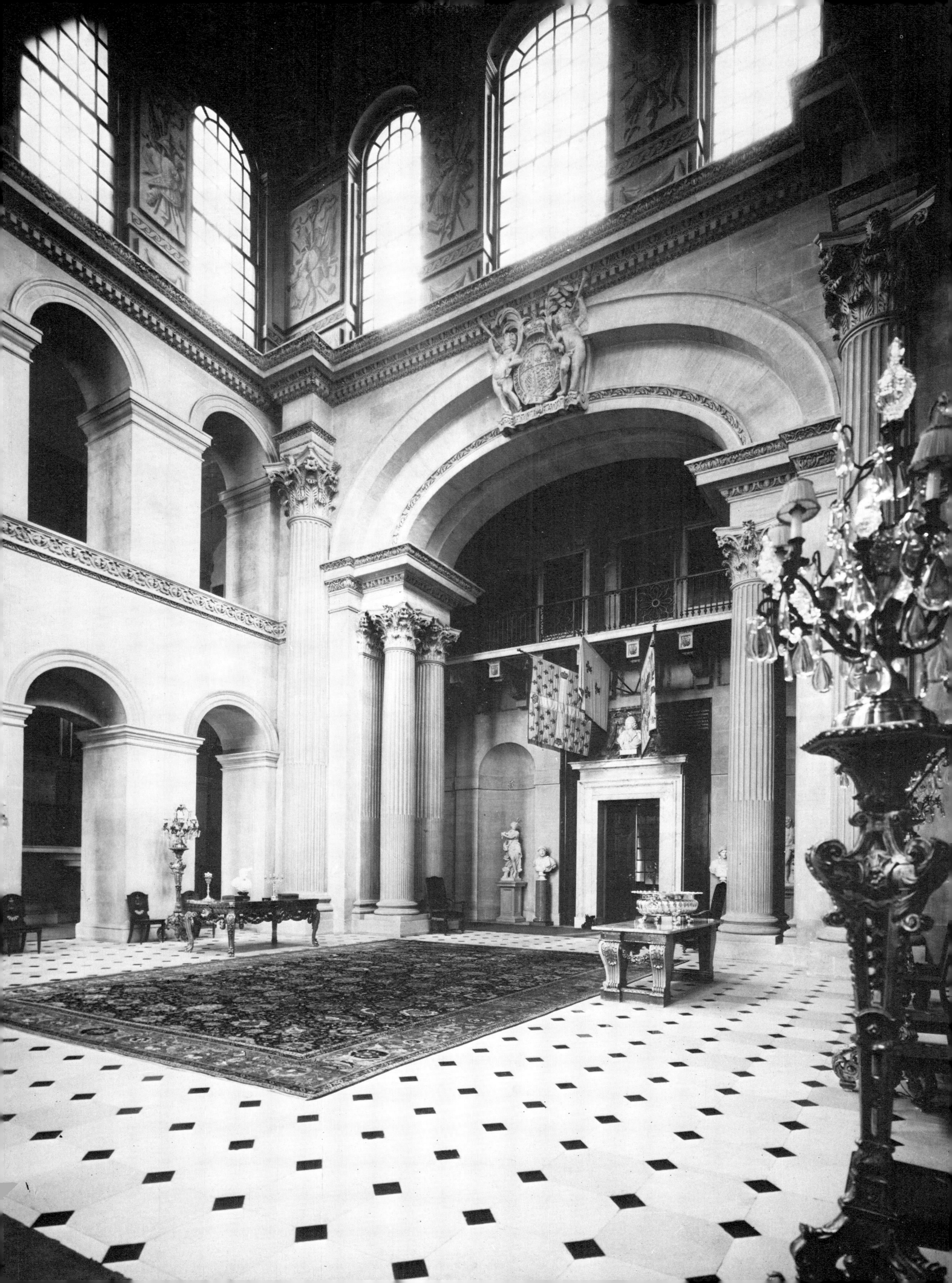

So there the Palace stands today: gigantic, magnificent, scarcely credible, built, improbably enough, upon what David Green has called a wild estate over sixty miles from London, and sketched first, it seems, upon the reverse side of a plan for the chapel at Greenwich on which Vanbrugh was also currently working in his capacity as Her Majesty's Comptroller at the Board of Works.

Basically, Vanbrugh's plan was clear-cut and clear to see. He wanted an even bigger and more splendid version of Castle Howard, the magnificent Yorkshire house he had built for Lord Carlisle*. Such a pile would be, above all, a monument to Marlborough's martial genius. Architect and client were at least agreed on that single and overriding objective. Domesticity was a secondary affair. Hence the statistics of magnificence.

Thus, from the beginning, we have this all-pervading sense of grandeur. The house is set well back upon a plateau above the Glyme valley, the enormous forecourt and containing wings are like a setting for a vast and unceasing theatrical occasion—undoubtedly Vanbrugh's intention—and help to make Blenheim one of the architectural wonders of Europe. 'Like a great college with a church in the middle,' as one eighteenth-century traveller recorded; a baroque palace, its likeness not to be found elsewhere in the world, thanks to the uncommon genius of Sir John.

Vanbrugh's approach to the private apartments at Blenheim was by way of a stately colonnade, now closed. The approach to the Duke's own quarters today is somewhat less diminishing to a visitor's self-esteem than the rest of this gigantic house. These 'little appartments,' as Vanbrugh called them, are set in behind the eastern quadrant of the North Front and entered via a small glazed door in the rusticated semi-basement storey. Within, after a sombre and somewhat constricted entrance hall, is a series of sizable but comfortable rooms. One door is labelled in small gold-leafed letterforms: DUKE'S SITTING-ROOM. The Duke sits at a well-ordered, high roll-top desk.

Early last year, John Albert Edward William Spencer-Churchill, His Grace the 10th Duke of Marlborough, Baron Spencer Earl of Sunderland, Baron Churchill, Earl of Marlborough, Marquis of Blandford, Prince of the Holy Roman Empire, etc, etc, had a rugged eight-hour operation which has left him, he says, somewhat less than fit.

Visitors who have seen him before are not easy to convince on this score. He walks with the aid of a stick, but he retains the pink complexion of the Churchills. He can command his two dogs to instant docility with an impressive snap in his voice. He is leaner than he was, but still, as a very tall man, keeps a straight back. Perhaps he moves with a new circumspection and lights up his pipe as if prepared for deeper reflection upon questions. Nevertheless, even whilst offering a not unduly tragic lament that he is now over seventy, he readily admits that he still finds Blenheim an extremely interesting place to live in and to organize, despite its manifold contemporary headaches. His major regret is that he can no longer hunt. He shoots and plays croquet: 'both old men's sports,' he says, smiling thinly.

Unlike many owners of historic houses he has been in ownership for quite some time. He inherited in 1934. 'My father died very suddenly. Very suddenly. At the time I was living in a Queen Anne house in Leicestershire in which I was very happy. My family was born there. I hunted regularly with the Quorn and the Cottesmore. I was thoroughly enjoying life when I found myself owner of Blenheim. It was rather a shock, I'll admit. I'd known it would come to me, but the suddenness was disturbing, to say the least. But one takes these things in one's stride, of course, and I soon began to take my place in local affairs. I was five times Mayor of Woodstock and that included the first year of the war. I'm also still on the Bench here, but

Opposite *Four aspects of Blenheim showing*, above, *part of the Great Court or North Forecourt and* below *the Water-terrace gardens with the Bernini Fountain in the foreground. Also shown is a view of the East front from the formal gardens and a section of the House, showing the architectural detail*

*See pp. 100—111

I'm no longer Chairman; I retired at seventy. One has to nowadays . . . a new law . . . probably just as well.'

'But you'd grown up here, presumably?'

'Of course, although I did have a somewhat divided life as a boy. My parents separated fairly early on in their marriage. I used to spend part of my holidays here and the rest in the South of France, or wherever my mother happened to be staying at the time. Then I became a soldier. After my marriage I made my own life elsewhere, as I've explained. But I'd been happy enough here as a boy. My memories of Blenheim go back a long way. Back to carriages and all that. I was reminded only the other day that exactly sixty years ago, towards the end of April, I set out as a boy of ten, complete with cricket-bag for the summer term, to go back to my private school—St Aubyns at Rottingdean. We set out for the station at Oxford but had to turn back after a couple of miles. By that time the carriage was stuck in the snow. We measured three feet of snow at Blenheim that April.'

'What else do you remember about pre-war Blenheim?'

'Well, I didn't have all that long, of course, before the war came, but I do recall one dance we had for my daughter Sarah here in 'thirty-nine. A great occasion: white ties, decorations, tiaras, the lot. And another just after the war for my grand-daughter. Everybody looked rather splendid. These things don't happen any more. The most you can hope for is black ties. I can't say I'm personally very sorry. I hate those stiff collars and studs, and probably couldn't put one on these days, but it did look rather splendid—the way everything and everyone used to look at the Opera at Covent Garden before the war. I still go when I can. Nowadays tweeds seem to be the thing. But the music hasn't suffered, which is the main thing.'

'What have been the most striking changes at Blenheim over the same period?'

'I suppose I can best sum up that by telling you that a couple of winters before the war I was told by one of my staff that to keep the house heated was taking a ton of coal a day. Nowadays, of course, one couldn't begin to do it. We use oil, anyway, and heat the main part of the house just before the visiting-season opens to dry out any of the State Rooms that seem a bit damp. I live in these quarters here and keep them pretty warm. I've needed the warmth this winter.'

'Did the house suffer much during the war?'

'Well, we took our share of punishment, although it could have been worse, I suppose. First, we had Malvern College here, then MI5 and then the American Southern Command. By that time I was back in uniform and acted as military liaison officer here with the Americans. We had a score or more of army huts in the Great Court and altogether it was a very different affair from an historic house. After the war the Office of Works moved in and set about repairing the ravages but it was a long job. We didn't really open to the public until nineteen-fifty.'

'How many visitors do you get now?'

'Last year we got one hundred and sixty-five thousand.'

'Do you mind having these visitors wandering around your home?'

'Well, one's always asked that and the truthful answer is that one's home is one's home. Nobody in his right mind willingly invites thousands of strangers into his home. But the other fact is that we need those visitors. They bring in about fifteen thousand pounds a year, and keeping this house in anything like reasonable order takes every penny of it. And we do rather pride ourselves on keeping Blenheim in good order—and clean. But there are other things. During the past ten years I've spent sixty thousand pounds of my own money on the stone-work alone, and the Government has spent an equal amount.'

'Vanbrugh's poor workmanship?'

'Not really. The stone came from a score of quarries, mostly local, and much of the stone which was used for the outside has turned out to be pretty soft. Masons didn't use cement in those days, as you probably know. In the course of time—over two hundred and fifty years—the iron ties which they used for linking the dressed stone have corroded and the stone has suffered in consequence. Not many people realize, I think, that the house and courts here cover over seven acres of ground. That's a lot of house to look after. That's why I need to plough back every penny I can into the house.'

'Presumably, it costs more than fifteen thousand a year to do that?'

'Well, we have other sources. A film company made part of Tommy Steele's film here. What's it called? "Half-a-Sixpence." That money went back into the house. But apart from all that I'd like to see a really good colour film made of the house. Blenheim deserves it. The colour here is magnificent. The tapestries alone would make it a worth-while venture.'

'What about BBC Two?'

'Well, I'm very impressed by their colour TV. I've watched it a good deal whilst recovering from this operation and a recent bout of flu. I like it.'

'Do you run Blenheim very much as a business?'

'Well, first and foremost, of course, it's my home. I've only a very small house in London. I really spend as much time here as I possibly can. But we do try to be efficient. Here are yesterday's figures. We try to see that the house is something worth visiting. The fact that it's a palace—and it certainly is—has a strong appeal for people, I think, don't you? After Sir Winston's death we had rather more visitors, of course. They seem to like to visit the churchyard at Bladon and then come on here where he was born. They can buy souvenirs. They seem to like to do that. Most of 'em seem to be able to spend money and most now come in their own cars. That can prove a disaster on a wet day. I've watched 'em carving up the grass. But there it is. I do wish, though, that they wouldn't leave the hand-brake on so often when they're taking off.'

'Do you have any side-shows here or whatever they're usually termed?'

'Not really. I think the house and Park are enough for most people. But we do try to keep a fairly lively programme going through the season. We recently had a ball and fashion parade in aid of Mountbatten's Soldiers, Sailors and Air Force fund and we also have the Churchill Memorial Concerts. We're far from moribund. Look at this list.'

The Duke crosses to a window overlooking the gardens. Pinned on one of the folded-back shutters is a list of the season's events. They range from rallies in the Park by the Pony Club, Guild of Lady Drivers and Rolls-Royce owners, to a Land Agents' and Surveyors' Centenary Ball in the Long Library. There has also been a water-ski show.

'Curious thing.' the Duke ruminates, back at his desk, 'the water-skiing isn't all that popular. I should have thought it would have been, wouldn't you? It must be a novelty in a place like this.'

'Don't you think most visitors still come because Blenheim itself is something so fantastic?'

'Maybe. Probably.'

'How much land do you have here?'

'Altogether about ten thousand acres. Most of it's now in the care of my son. He lives nearby and that's mainly his responsibility. But I keep a watchful eye—with a bailiff—on three thousand acres separately in the Park. I'm currently very interested in the prospects of barley-fed cattle. I can't say I like the taste of barley-fed beef myself, but it seems very popular. The cattle are fed fairly scientifically and don't spend any time outdoors. It's

Opposite, above *The Long Library, looking north towards the Willis organ*
Below *The three State Rooms, leading out of the Saloon, are hung with tapestries of Marlborough's campaigns*

rather a new thing and it interests me.'

'Forestry?'

'Well, we do a fair amount of planting and so on. I'm more concerned with what we lose. We lost quite a few in last year's snow. One of the branches of that cedar you see out there was absolutely weighed right down with the weight of snow it was carrying. I was certain it would snap off, big as it is. The gardeners couldn't reach it by ladder. Fortunately, the thaw got going in time. What really worries me is the way some of our beeches here seem to be getting diseased. Trees are a great pleasure but they do

Above *The Green Drawing-Room. Above the fireplace hangs a portrait of the fourth Duke and on the wall on the left can be seen a painting by Reynolds of his Duchess Caroline*
Opposite *The Red Drawing-Room; at the far end hangs a painting by Sargent of Charles, 9th Duke of Marlborough, and family (the present Duke is standing between his mother and father)*

Opposite *The Saloon, with murals by Laguerre and marble doorways by Grinling Gibbons*
Above *Another view of the Long Library designed by Vanbrugh as a picture gallery, but adapted later by Hawksmoor to a library*

need a lot of looking after.'

'Do you think a place like Blenheim has any future?'

'I just don't know. As I've said, I've tried to make arrangements for my own son to be able to take it over and run it, but what he can do about *his* son is a very different matter. Every kind of new tax seems to make the possibility more difficult and problematical. One picks up the papers these days and really one begins to wonder whether the world any of us has known can last much longer.'

With that somewhat gloomy observation His Grace rises from the roll-top desk, picks up his stick and wanders slowly out into the corridor towards his secretary's office, preoccupied with, but not overwhelmed by, the problems of keeping the largest private house in Britain as private as twentieth-century Britain will allow.

KEDLESTON HALL

'ALL DESIGNED by Adam in the best taste.' So wrote Horace Walpole after viewing Lord Scarsdale's completed Kedleston, adding somewhat acidly that it was 'too expensive for his estate.'

Despite the fact that Kedleston seems a supreme architectural demonstration of the unity of purpose that can occasionally fuse the minds of two men of vastly different backgrounds and temperament—in this instance, Nathaniel Curzon, first Baron Lord Scarsdale and Robert Adam—the house is, nevertheless, the work of three architects of whom Adam was the last.

Curzon's first architect was Matthew Brettingham who was responsible for the essential structure we see today: a central block with two wings, connected by curving corridors. Indeed, Brettingham started on the project in 1758 and under his direction, the north-east wing, which was—and still is—the family's living-quarters, was completed.

How James Paine came into the picture and succeeded Brettingham remains a somewhat hazy picture. Perhaps the reason was simply that Paine was the most successful architect of his time and Curzon had to be abreast of aesthetic fashions at all cost. Whatever the reason, Paine prepared fresh designs for the whole building and supervised, between 1757 and 1761, the building of the North Front of the central block.

Then, in turn, Paine was supplanted by Adam, who was already preparing designs for the interior decoration of the house. Existing records suggest that Paine was not willing to relinquish the job to the younger man; certainly he made handsome acknowledgement of Adam's skills and the two men remained friends, a rare enough occurrence amongst architects in those competitive times.

Kedleston thus shows a comparison of the work of two great architects in the clearest possible terms: the North Front by Paine; the South by Adam: the first a demonstration of the then-current ideas concerning the 'correct' interpretation of the Palladian ideal, the latter demonstrating the virtues of 'movement'—that coinage of Vanbrugh's which reappears from time to time to enliven a style becoming too set in its ways.

Between 1765 and 1770 innovations were magnificently carried out, the sense of movement being established by the curving staircase as a splendid foil for the great dome. Had flanking wings been built on this side, too, the total effect would have been as magnificent as that of any great house in Europe. Adam did, however, complete his plans for the decoration of the interior, and the staterooms at Kedleston show his genius in full measure. Here are decorative schemes of immense imaginative power. The result is a series of rooms of palatial splendour, but wholly lacking in pomposity.

Opposite *The Saloon with coffered dome rising to sixty-two feet*

THANKS TO the foresight of its eighteenth-century sponsor, Nathaniel Curzon, fifth Baronet, later Lord Scarsdale, and his three architects, and latterly, to the wishes of its present owner, Kedleston remains amongst the most private of Britain's Stately Homes.

There are two approaches to the house: first, the main entrance from the Derby-Kedleston road, leading to Quarndon, Weston Underwood and Hulland. Here, past the Adam lodge and magnificent 1760 iron gates (by Bakewell) set beneath a fine arch, thence, by the handsome bridge, also by Adam, spanning the Kedleston lakes.

But there is another, lesser-known entrance offering unexpected charms, this time from the Derby-Ashbourne Road, and despite the careful guidelines of the one-inch Ordance Survey, the visitor is still apt to come upon this entrance suddenly and unexpectedly. Two toy-like lodges, flanking modest iron gates, are set casually at a turn in a Derbyshire lane, two miles off the A52, five miles out from industrial Derby, going north-west towards Ashbourne, that strangely forlorn yet architecturally exciting town at the edge of the peak National Park.

Beyond the gates, the mile-long approach is through handsome but casually-tended parkland. The house remains hidden until the last curve in the drive, as if determined to keep within the shelter of its well-timbered background.

Then, and only then, is the famous North Front of the house revealed: a palatial façade with a great Corinthian portico, flattened dome and flanking wings. But even then it is only from behind a forecourt enclosed within a decorative iron grille.

From the steps of the house, an unspoiled panorama is to be seen: a lake, seemingly without limit, spanned by the bridge that Adam designed, and beyond the undulating timbered slopes of the Derbyshire countryside —with not a rooftop to intrude.

This sense of privacy, so marked in the setting of Kedleston, is sedulously cultivated, despite the fierce competition amongst the top contenders in the Stately Homes League. Kedleston is open only on Sunday afternoons and Bank Holidays, content to remain a private house with palace appended, as it were.

This rare and pervasive privacy may possibly derive from Nathaniel Curzon's determination to have a family house built before a start was made on the great house. Most of the great Whig builders, only too keenly aware of their own mortality, pressed on regardless. Their exigent haste was understandable but too frequently brought them sharply up against cheerless alternatives. On the one hand they could suffer considerable discomfort if they wished to be on the site: on the other, they suffered miseries of frustration trying to supervise the building of their palaces if they stayed in their London houses, appearing only infrequently during the summer building season. Not so Sir Nathaniel. In his insistence upon the logic and comfort of the leisurely approach he differed emphatically from the nabobs of his time bitten by the building bug.

That he was a patron of uncommon knowledge and authoritarian impulse is shown by his dealings with the three architects who helped him to build his palace; also by the fact that he demolished and rebuilt a village to get the site he wanted; above all, by the great house he commissioned and in the design of which he was plainly a force to be reckoned with at every stage.

Viscount and Lady Scarsdale
Opposite *The boathouse designed by Robert Adam*

The North Front, the design of James Paine, was built between 1757 and 1761

Little wonder then that he commissioned a comfortable Palladian family mansion planned from the beginning to become an important element in the grand design.

This mansion—for it is no mere pavilion—remains today as the family house, lived in, year-round, by Lord Scarsdale and his wife, on exactly the same site as earlier houses that the family have lived in for well over eight hundred years. Seventeenth-century records in the British Museum cite a front door and porch already five hundred years old in the then-existent house and its Great Hall and Buttery. That house was pulled down in 1698 and replaced by a large brick and stone mansion, built for

the 2nd Baronet by Smith of Warwick. This house was in turn demolished to make way for the great house we see today.

Richard Nathaniel Curzon, Viscount Scarsdale, the present owner of the Kedleston domain, is an upright, broad-shouldered man above middle height, with very much an outdoor look about him. He is seventy this year, but, in corduroy windcheater, heavy slacks and suede bootees, descending in lively manner from a Land-Rover, he looks a decade younger. He currently laments that he's by no means as fit as he'd like to be, but his tan belies his dirge.

He has the consular Curzon profile so well-suited to ancient Roman coinage; but here the imperious outline is enlivened by ready laughter. Nor has it been impaired in any nuance by a lively career as an amateur middle-weight boxer, a sporting interest maintained in his present vice-presidency and stewardship of the British Boxing Board of Control. He takes his stewardship extremely seriously, coming to London for monthly meetings—but returning forthwith to Derbyshire. He is as well-informed about the worth of any British professional boxer as any sports writer. He discusses these men and matters with lively interest and academic detachment.

Kedleston, apart from his well-disciplined boxing and business interests, is his whole life. Unlike the owners of many Stately Homes he lives in his and wouldn't dream of commuting from an all-mod-con town house to a weekend demi-semi-rural life. 'I'm a countryman,' he explains. 'Hunting and shooting and the way of life in the country have been my lifelong interests. There's little enough to keep me in London. I like being here.'

Has that been his view ever since inheriting Kedleston?

'In the main, yes. I never cease telling myself how lucky I am to be here,' he says disarmingly. 'I never expected it to be mine. When it came to me I was surprised. But from then on it became my major interest in life. With a modicum of luck I shall be able to leave the house and six-thousand-acre estate in a better state than I found it—and that's something fairly unusual these days with a place like this on one's hands—as I think you'll agree.'

'True enough, but how literally can one take your remark that you never expected Kedleston to be yours?'

'Quite literally. I was the son of a younger brother. The elder brother was, as you probably know, the redoubtable Lord Curzon, Viceroy of India and all the rest. Between his high State appointments—he was also Foreign Secretary and a member of the War Cabinet in the First War—he spent as much time here as he could, after he succeeded in 1916 from his father, the 4th Baron Scarsdale, but obviously it was a broken kind of existence. He was married twice, and one naturally assumed he'd be likely to have an heir. In any case I was too busy trying to make my own way—and making my own mistakes—to bother overmuch about inheriting Kedleston.'

'But you knew the house quite well?'

'Very well indeed. My father lived at Weston, about two miles away, in one of the estate houses. On holidays from school I used to come over to Kedleston most Sundays, walking here across the fields. I enjoyed walking and I liked Kedleston. I knew every acre of the estate—which was then ten thousand acres—having shot game and ridden my horses over all of it, I knew every wood, every stream. My father was a great tutor and beloved, like any grandfather, by all our tenants and employees.'

'Did you like your uncle? He seems to have been a difficult man by all accounts.'

'Of course I liked him, and one can't help but admire any man who started by correcting his Latin tutor at Eton. He was brilliant but difficult, as I learned from personal experience. I need hardly tell you that he could be a very intimidating person to a young man. One encounter with him was far from happy.'

'Concerning the house?'

'No, that was never mentioned. Chiefly about my career, or, rather, careers. After Sandhurst I went into the Royal Scots Greys, in 1918. At

The Marble Hall lined with twenty veined alabaster columns

the end of the First War I learned that my regiment was likely to be sent to India for twelve years. At any time in one's life, a dozen years can seem like a lifetime, particularly to someone in his early twenties with an eye for the pretty girls. Some of my contemporaries decided to leave the army. After due reflection I decided to do the same. For me it was a mistake. I loved the army and I didn't realize at the time that my friends had names that took them straight into good jobs in the City. I remember an interview with my uncle in September nineteen-twenty, soon after my father had died, at Number One Carlton House Terrace, his London house. He did not want me to stay on in the army, as India at that time was a fairly expensive affair for a young officer in a fashionable regiment, and I wasn't at all well-off. And it was plain he was in no mood to help. Anyway, we began to disagree. At one point I said he hadn't helped my father overmuch by giving him notice to quit the family house where we'd lived for twenty years or more, in favour of a new estate manager in 1916 when my grandfather had died. Not the most discreet of remarks for a young man to make but, then, young men are rarely discreet. His eyes filled with tears. He had been very fond of my father who was only a year younger than himself. He rang the bell and had me shown out of his sitting-room. My uncle certainly had his more high-handed and less endearing moments. Yet, I admired him.'

'Did you leave the army?'

'I did indeed. I went into the aircraft industry—the Aircraft Manufacturing Company which later became de Havillands—as an apprentice. I'd always been fascinated by aircraft and flying, and at one time had seriously considered joining the Royal Flying Corps as the RAF was then known. But what I hadn't reckoned on—like many others—was that the industry was then in process of being run down after the war. I stayed on, hoping against hope the tide would turn. I thoroughly enjoyed my life as a fitter. I was airborne quite a bit, flying as a technical type and so on, but finally I could see there was no future in it.'

'What then?'

'My uncle—perhaps as some kind of peace-offering—got me a job as assistant to an estate manager, Mr Paine Galway, at Belvoir Castle in Leicestershire. I had a splendid life on a shoe-string. One could in those days. Hunting two or three days a week, trips to London, parties and so on. And all the time I was learning a job which has been useful to me ever since. It's possible, of course, that my uncle had got me the job as some kind of preparation for taking over Kedleston, but it still didn't occur to me. After all, in 1917 he'd married again and might still have had a son. He wasn't more than sixty at the time.'

'And then?'

'I suppose I could have got myself a place in estate management, but I was restless. After a bit of string-pulling with the late Lord Vansittart of the Foreign Office I went off to Rome as an honorary attaché—with my Derbyshire Yeomanry full dress uniform—much to my uncle's annoyance again as he hadn't been consulted. His annoyance turned to fury when I wished to marry someone he hadn't vetted, so to speak. Anyway I did marry the lady, resigned from the embassy staff, returned to London and set about making my way, somewhat improbably, as a West India merchant. Whether I'd have made my fortune is another matter. Within a year my uncle was dead. He died quite suddenly—still only in his mid-sixties—and I was the owner of Kedleston.'

'When was that?'

'In nineteen-twenty-five. So I've been here well over forty years. You may find it difficult to believe, but it was a wholly unexpected situation

Opposite, above left *The Doric doorcase in the Library (seen also above top) surmounted by a small, oval painting by Van Dyck*
Right *The State Bed, designed by Adam, with cedar of Lebanon posts carved in the form of palm trunks*
Below, left *The State Boudoir is partially divided by a screen of columns; the painting above the fireplace is by Hone; a detail of the looking-glass is seen above*
Right *An alcove in the State Dining-Room with curved tables specially designed by Adam*

for me and I was totally unprepared for it. If I'd been a more far-sighted type I suppose I'd have been able to move straight in with all plans ready.'

'But you had no qualms?'

'Indeed I had. The very first week I was asked to find the cash for wages for the entire estate staff. I hadn't a bean. Anyway, I pulled through with the help of the estates' bank and a loan and gradually began to find my feet.'

'And enjoyed it ever since?'

'Always. Not a single regret. And always—as I said—with the fullest possible realization of my good fortune. After all, I live here in this marvellous house, overlooking some of the finest country in the world and with eight square miles of England in my care. Who wouldn't count himself lucky on those terms?'

'Do you farm yourself?'

'No, we have about twenty farms at Kedleston, none above five hundred acres. I take a great interest in them, obviously, and know all my tenants well. One has to. All are friends. Several are second and third generations, as are several members of the estate staff. That kind of continuity makes for a sense of security and stability on both sides. I know it's fashionable these days to decry these things. Feudal and all that—which is nonsense. I think such relationships can be valuable. Maybe I'm prejudiced.'

'What happened to Kedleston during the war?'

'Personally, I wasn't greatly involved. I was back in a war again, mostly in the Middle East. I had been in the Territorial Army since 1920—I received my Territorial Decoration in 1939. Before I left for Egypt in 1941 I had offered part of the house and part of the park to the War Office, and by 1941 army units were encamped here.'

Opposite *The Music Room to the east of the Marble Hall contains many paintings, which include 'The triumph of Bacchus' by Giordano*
Above *Suits of armour in the Tapestry Corridor*

'And after the war?'

'My life changed somewhat. We had so much to do here. I married again and my wife began to take a great interest in Kedleston, particularly in estate management and the furnishings and decoration. We still have all the Adam drawings, of course, and can thus consult his ideas when it comes to a question of redecorating and so on. Which is just as well, for as you probably know, some of his ideas for colour schemes were extremely personal and unusual and subtle to a degree.'

'Do you mind opening the house to the public?'

'I don't think we find it a burden of any consequence. It must be remembered that it makes money. It's an historic and beautiful house which people do want to see and our privacy is well-looked after in this family wing. Then again, we only open on Sundays and Bank Holidays from Easter to the end of September, so we aren't really in any kind of rat race. Fortunately, if we want to sunbathe on the terrace, we can most days.'

'Do you get many visitors?'

'Not by the usual Stately Homes standards. Between five and six hundred on Sundays, more on Bank Holidays.'

'And you don't find it gets you down?'

'By the end of the season it's becoming a bit of a strain, but that's because we both have to take so personal an interest in the house. My wife looks after visitors and is generally in charge. She also, as I said, looks after all the refurbishing and supervises all the repainting and work in the gardens. All her planning and replanting have been a great success.'

'Running Kedleston is, presumably, a fairly costly business?'

'It can be—in both big and small ways. For instance, I sent a chair away to have a leg mended. The quotation was eighty-five pounds. When I suggested this seemed a bit steep I was told the chair was one of a set made by Daniel Marot and worth anything up to and beyond a thousand pounds apiece. Heirlooms can be pretty costly items to have around when they begin to age.'

'What about the upkeep generally?'

'I've always tried to pace the expenditure to work within a budget I can afford, but sometimes one comes up against some really terrifying items. For example, the whole place has got to be rewired electrically and that I'm told, on sound authority, will cost around ten thousand pounds. All on something that won't be seen or appreciated by the public. That kind of news can be rather galling.'

'Couldn't you sell a minor master to pay for the wiring? Mightn't it seem a reasonable exchange at a time like this?'

'It would perhaps, but unfortunately Kedleston's possessions are entailed. I can't sell a chair just like that to pay for a new carpet or to clean the stonework or even for something as imperative as a new wiring system. I can sell timber from the woodlands and use the cash at my own discretion, but I can't sell a thing in the house. That's something that most people don't realize. I suppose it makes sense, as otherwise I could not have inherited such magnificent pictures, furniture and so on. But as running-costs spiral whilst the possessions get more and more valuable, and probable death duties go mounting up, it's difficult for someone in my position to be wildly enthusiastic about the situation. I have the headaches. But let's have a look at the possessions.'

Kedleston's owner gets up from the sofa and leads the way out of his private sitting-room, via one of the quadrant galleries, into the great house.

In these utilitarian days it is impossible for most people to begin to comprehend the consummate confidence of Sir Nathaniel and his fellow Whigs who could contemplate the building of such a house as Kedleston. Yet, as the English countryside still affirms, scores of them did, without apparently, taking undue heed of the future. There would always be that kind of England.

Garden pavilion near the swimming pool

Opposite *Venetian window and pedimented doorcase in the State Drawing-Room. The chandelier is of Waterford crystal*

Yet even to the architectural enthusiast who has seen Kedleston before, the visual splendour of the Great Hall, with its twenty 25-foot columns of Derbyshire alabaster, each two feet six inches in diameter, is still a near-awesome sight. As if this were not enough, there is also the circular Saloon, one of the most beautiful rooms in the world, and certainly the most beautiful room designed by Robert Adam and decorated, under his direction, by a team of craftsmen, including grisailles by Rebecca, paintings by William Hamilton and a set of cast iron 'altar' stoves devised by Adam himself for heating this sizable chamber, over forty feet in diameter and sixty-four feet to the topmost point of the dome.

Set on either side of the axis established by Great Hall and Saloon are the State Rooms: Drawing-Room, Dining-Room, Music Room, Library and the State Bedroom with its attendant Boudoir.

The furniture and decorative details of Kedleston are of equal splendour, scarcely to be rivalled in any royal palace: from the green Derbyshire alabaster Venetian window and doorway of the Drawing-Room to the much-documented rococo sofas with their gilded dolphin feet; from the palm-tree posts of the four-poster State Bed, hung with silver lace, to the beautiful chimneypieces to be seen throughout the house. Here at Kedleston, Adam had the chance of a lifetime and took it—to the limit. Here he came closest to realizing all those ambitions in building and decoration for which his early training, wide experience and assured and certain taste had prepared him. He wasn't allowed full scope. Even Sir Nathaniel's vast ambitions had to be encompassed within some kind of budget, however flexible, but he came as close as ever he did, notwithstanding his masterly work at Syon.

WESTON PARK

WESTON is built on the site of the original manor-house, the property of the Weston and Mytton families. The last of the Myttons, Elizabeth, was, remarkably enough, the architect of the present house; "an ambitious stone and brick elevation of eleven bays and three storeys".*

Elizabeth Mytton married, in 1651 at the age of twenty, Sir Thomas Wilbraham, of Woodhey in Cheshire. Twenty years later she demolished the existing gabled house and then designed and supervised the building of one of the most historic seventeenth-century houses in England, ranking with Sudbury in Derbyshire and Raynham in Norfolk as examples of outstanding houses of the seventeenth century designed by amateurs.

The house was started in 1671; in 1688 a stable block was added and, as if these domestic architectural activities were not enough for her energies, in 1700 Lady Wilbraham rebuilt the medieval church of Weston, restraining her delight in originality sufficiently to retain the original tower. (The church, the parish church, was restored and enlarged in 1876.)

During the eighteenth century the ownership of Weston passed first to the Newports, Earls of Bradford, and in 1762 to the Bridgemans, an old Devon family with a seat, nevertheless, at Castle Bromwich in Warwickshire. The earldom of Bradford was revived in favour of the Bridgeman family in 1815. The first Bridgeman owner was responsible for the layout of the parkland and gardens, which remain substantially as they were then planned. He also erected, to the north-east of the house, the impressive group of farm buildings.

Almost every successive owner of Weston has made changes. The second earl stuccoed the house. The third earl, upon his succession in 1865, reorientated it from south to east, added a new porch and wing, made a billiard room in part of an old internal courtyard and heightened the dining room. The fourth added the present main staircase and a smoking room in the remainder of the courtyard. The fifth removed the stucco just before the second World War and brought the original red brick-work happily to light again. The present Earl and Countess have sought successfully to restore to the interior of the house the usual pleasures of 1671.

Opposite *The East Front, now the main entrance front, of Weston Park*

**English Country Houses: Caroline* by John Comforth and Oliver Hill (Country Life).

The Earl of Bradford
Opposite, above *The admirably-proportioned Drawing-Room has been enhanced by the skilful use of colour*
Below *The Tapestry Room in which the colour and texture of the fine eighteenth-century Gobelin tapestries remain unimpaired*

WESTON PARK lies hidden within its vast acreage off the busy London-Holyhead (A5) road, near the curiously-named Staffordshire village of Weston-under-Lizard.

An intending visitor might easily overshoot the lodges at the entrance were it not for the pale-blue-painted board which announces the appropriate times for viewing Weston.

The house lies deep within its parkland, landscaped by Capability Brown. Even after the long drive has been negotiated the house still seems reluctant to be revealed. Then the pink brick façade with its stone dressings and segmental gables comes into view. The drive sweeps round into a gravelled courtyard faced by the brick-and-stone east front, sturdily guarded by a pillared Victorian *porte cochere*.

The house has always aroused the interest of its successive owners and prompted challenges to change the *status quo*. But the present owners have had the toughest job of all, for they set about their task after two world wars had changed a great deal of the English way of life, diminished family fortunes, cut down the availability of staff, raised wages ten-fold, and, generally, made most Stately Homes into fearsome white elephants.

Lord Bradford, in his late fifties, a compact, military-looking man with greying hair and clipped grey moustache, makes no bones about the fact that Weston is a white elephant. Yet he never uses the term regretfully or apprehensively, but, almost genially, as if welcoming the challenge of ownership in straitened times. He is plainly a man of energy, enterprise and resolution and has quietly and carefully set about the task of making his white elephant not too elephantine in the second half of the twentieth century. He hasn't rushed things, which means, as is usual with such men, that he has done more than many of the would-be thrusters.

For a start: few owners have dealt so logically and painlessly with the problems of twentieth-century living in a Stately Home. 'Weston has been the base of my life—a place I've always wanted to come back to, a place I couldn't think of abandoning although, of course, such possibilities inevitably cross one's mind at times. But if one likes a way of life well enough one has to work out ways and means of keeping things as close as possible to what one likes. Circumstances change, of course, but one likes to think that one is resilient enough to change to meet them. I grew up here as a boy. When I married—after the war, that is—my father offered us the top floor. We took it and after his death we stayed up here. It makes more sense. There was no point in trying to run the house as he and his parents had run the place. We're very comfortable upstairs. The nursery and schoolroom were up here, so we live close to the children, we're insulated from the public down below, and we certainly get the best views.'

He crosses to the window and it is easy to see that some changes in the patrician way of life enforced by the twentieth century can have some very pleasant visual compensations. Below, the formal gardens open out on to a wide parkland, beautiful and serene. Once upon a recent time the children of the house enjoyed this splendid panorama—if they had time. Now the vistas belong to the owner, who moves an arm to take in the woods that Capability Brown planned for his great-great-grandfather, the curving lake at one end of the arc, James Paine's Temple of Diana at the other. It is an outlook of enduring and improbable splendour for this day and age.

'On a fine day we see the Shropshire Hills,' Lord Bradford continues. 'Difficult to realize that Wolverhampton is less than ten miles away behind those trees, don't you think?'

The top floor is, fortunately, only the third storey of this great house with its surprisingly modest elevations. At least one Stately Home was designed, it seems, *not* to dwarf human scale. Perhaps the fact that Weston was designed by a woman also has a good deal to do with its unaggressive façades. Lady Wilbraham, depicted by Lely in one of a notable group of family portraits in the house, was a seventeenth-century chatelaine who chose to be the architect of her own house: she was also responsible for the church and stables. She was undoubtedly a lady of authority, energy and pertinacity, and, like all those possessed by a fever for building—from Bess of Hardwick to the King Ludwig—was always in the middle of some new architectural enterprise. Weston would seem a life's work for most amateur architects, but Lady Wilbraham was also building at her husband's house at Woodhey in Cheshire.

She was born Elizabeth Mytton in 1632, heiress of Weston, and married Sir Thomas Wilbraham, owner of Woodhey, at the age of twenty and scarcely stopped building thereafter. She was certainly a scholarly architect, consulting the most correct sources for her inspiration. Her annotated copy of the first English translation of the first volume of Palladio's *Quattro libri del'architettura* is still preserved in the library, with her beautiful calligraphy on the endpapers listing current charges for marble, paint and the

Opposite, above *The Marble Hall leads off from the Entrance Hall and is Italianate in feeling with its distinctive black-and-white flagged marble floor. The white marble staircase with delicate wrought-ironwork dates from the end of the last century*
Below *The newly-decorated Dining-Room now forms a magnificent setting for the collection of larger portraits*

rest of the building impedimenta with which she was plainly enjoying herself at the time. She was clearly not to be hoodwinked, as witness a memorandum of a bargain with Sir William Wilson, the sculptor, for setting up four monuments, '2 of the Better, 2 of the Worser, sort and for finding alaplaster and marble £23'. She also refers to the relative cost of 'alaplaster' and marble, and of gold lettering on black marble which cost a farthing more than black lettering on white marble. Yet the face in the Lely portrait is far from that of a Carolingian blue-stocking. Forceful, certainly, but the eyes have more than a hint of worldly merriment about them. Her husband, whose portrait hangs in the dining-room, has a genially cynical air about him as if reconciled to the hectic life occasioned by his wife's enterprises so long as his hunting and shooting weren't unduly hindered by those unfeminine activities.

The house built by Lady Wilbraham is certainly commodious but not overpoweringly so. Despite Lord Bradford's references to Weston as a 'white elephant of a place', few Stately Homes offer so many thousands of visitors a series of State Rooms so sympathetically proportioned, detailed —and now restored, redecorated and maintained.

'All that is my wife's work,' the owner says with a touch of pride. She's made a marvellous job of getting rid of the worst of the Victorian excesses. She's also got an unusual feeling for colour and I'm only too glad and willing to let her go ahead. Judging by remarks from the visitors, they approve too.'

'Who did the actual painting?'

'We did a large part of it with our own staff, but in the latest series of redecorations the strain was too great, and Jackson's of Hammersmith took over and did a fine job. Our own painters have done a tremendous lot of very good work in the house, and there's always plenty more.'

'Presumably for other craftsmen too?'

'Any number we could afford. But it's astonishing how almost everyone has something to offer. My Irish butler, Bill Donaghy, for instance, has an unusual talent for bringing the best out of ormolu. As we've a fair number of French pieces here, that's a particularly useful talent. He also takes a great pride in keeping the silver in perfect condition, and will turn his hand to anything, including wine-making.'

Few owners of Stately Homes make their way around their treasures with so appreciative an eye, for Lord Bradford has both enthusiasm and detachment concerning his possessions. He owns them but is plainly not owned by them. He also knows every square inch of his house, which, thanks to the combined labours of himself and his wife, looks as if the rigours of the twentieth century are being kept well at bay. He has known his furniture and paintings all his life and watched the attributions of many of them grow more substantial as art historians have become more erudite and confident. The provenance of some once-suspect Van Dycks in the house is now indisputable, notably a portrait of Thomas Killigrew, a friend of Charles II. Until 1963, this portrait was generally accepted as a copy. Then expert cleaning and restoration established the priority and authenticity of the Weston portrait, a fine study in dichotomous arrogance and weakness. Similar stories of restoration and the establishing of authentic attribution are associated with other Van Dycks in the house; also with an outstanding painting by Jacopo Bassano, *The Way to Golgotha.*

Lord Bradford recounts these ups and downs of attribution with relish. He is extremely detached about it all. Of the Bassano he says: 'It was rather overlooked, labelled Veronese, for a couple of hundred years. Then it was cleaned by Horace Buttery and sent to an exhibition at the Royal Academy. While it was there the Director of the Rijksmuseum of Amsterdam,

Dr. van Schendel, recognized it as a painting given by the Dutch people to Charles the Second on his marriage. He told me the painting had been 'lost' for a couple of centuries and that the rediscovery gave him one of the most exciting days of his life. I don't know how it got there, but I was very glad to fall in with his wishes to exhibit the painting in Amsterdam.' Lord Bradford's particular pleasure amongst his paintings, however, is the works of noted sporting artists. Several of his special favourites hang in the fine hall, including a magnificent Stubbs, showing grey and brown horses in landscape with lake and trees, and an exuberant Ferneley, *Mr. Massey Stanley with cabriolet and hacks at Hyde Park Corner*, which captures to the full the self-confidence of Regency London. One group is of especial charm; half-a-dozen paintings by George Morland, depicting various stages in a day's hunting. These paintings are rendered in an impressionistic technique with cloud patterns that have much in common with the finest of Constable's smaller landscapes.

Weston has a double hall: the Entrance Hall and the Marble Hall, which encompasses the handsome staircase, an infiltration of uncommon distinction made by the 4th Earl in 1898 which might well fault many an architectural mandarin in its dating.

To the leisurely perambulator with an interest in furniture Weston offers what must be one of the country's most versatile collections of chairs. These sets range from eighteenth-century painted wheelbacks of delicate and frivolous charm to robust no-nonsense Georgian armchairs with firmly-planted, wide-spreading cabriole legs and arms well placed to take the forearms of a Bradford laying down the law. The house may well have witnessed such opinings in the past, for the family has included one of the most eminent of English lawyers who must also have been a sophisticated worldling. Sir Orlando Bridgeman, a staunch royalist, nevertheless managed to build up a lucrative conveyancing practice in forfeited lands during the Commonwealth. Yet, after the Restoration, he was chosen to preside at the trial of the regicides of Charles I. A tight-rope walker, indeed. 'The only disappointment he seems to have suffered in a highly successful career,' adds Lord Bradford, 'was that although he was made Lord Keeper of the Great Seal he was denied the title of Lord Chancellor which normally went with it. I daresay he was very disappointed but I've never regarded him as a particularly disappointed man, and I doubt whether he saw himself as one. I think he was far too shrewd a man of the world for that kind of regret. But he must have been a formidable personality. He was dismissed from office for refusing to set the seal to grants and pensions to the Royal mistresses. We've two portraits of him here.'

Riley's portrait of Sir Orlando hangs in the library above the chimney-piece and his bag of the Great Seal, now incorporated within a fire screen, stands below the portrait. Sir Orlando stares from the portrait: a forceful, firm-eyed man with long hair and down-turning moustache who would, the viewer feels, have been very much at home in the middle of high events at any time in English history, particularly our own.

Weston has close associations of a different order with another of Britain's most sophisticated men of high affairs. Weston possesses over a thousand letters written by Disraeli, then Prime Minister and a widower in his seventies, to Selina, wife of the 3rd Earl of Bradford, between 1873 and his death eight years later. Disraeli was a frequent visitor to Weston Park and dearly loved this great house with 'its scenes so fair'. His letters make a remarkable collection and several are displayed in a case in the West Marble Hall.

The Library is a dark warm room *en suite* with the Drawing Room, a beautifully proportioned room, with a fine plaster ceiling decorated in

Opposite, top and centre *The Temple of Diana, designed by James Paine, is a magnificent example of Georgian garden architecture*
Below *Looking from the Temple across the parkland towards the East Front of the house*

delicate pastel colours. Lady Bradford has the notion to give these two rooms a decorative unity by lightening the tones of the Library. For once her husband is less enthusiastic. He plainly prefers the darker tones of the painted shelves and leather bindings. 'So far, I've given my wife her head in all her decorative ideas,' Lord Bradford says wryly, 'but I've one or two reservations about the Library. I can see it would make a magnificent pair of rooms, especially as they open into each other and both rooms have these fine Corinthian supporting columns. But I find the Library as it is a particularly comfortable and relaxing room. Anyway, we'll see.'

The Library houses some extremely rare books, including editions of Redoute, Gould, Piranesi and Lord Bradford's particular pleasure: an uninterrupted run of Curtis's *Botanical Magazine* from 1787 until the present day.

Perhaps the most striking of the newly decorated rooms are the Dining Room, with its magnificent series of portraits, the Breakfast Room, now transformed into a small portrait gallery with warm red damask walls and curtains as a perfect foil for the paintings, and the beautifully-proportioned Drawing Room, with its fine plaster ceiling and Grecian columns decorated in pastel greens and yellows.

The colourful Tapestry Room has a fine set of eighteenth-century Gobelin tapestries which are unimpaired by time. The First Salon, too, has two beautiful tapestries (here they are Aubusson) depicting Spring and Winter.

Does Lord Bradford mind thousands of other people wandering through his house?

'Not at all. They help us to live here and I think they enjoy coming. After all, we don't offer them anything but the house and the park. We do have a minuscule fairground for the children, and a pets' corner, but that's the limit. No, I don't think I mind at all, and it's a marvellous place for people in places like Birmingham and Wolverhampton to be able to escape to.'

'How large is Weston?'

'About fourteen thousand acres, which includes fifty farms. My own major interests are farming and forestry. I like to get out early in the mornings up in the woods and do various jobs myself. I've an experimental area of woodland where I can work out my own theories, also other forestry interests up in Invernesshire and down in Devon and Cornwall, in the Tamar Valley. They take up a lot of my time.'

'Plus a good deal of committee work?'

'Well, I was President of the Country Landowners Association, and later of the Timber Growers' Organization. Also I was Chairman of the Forestry Committee of Great Britain and a Crown Estate Commissioner, and I sat on many other national and local committees. But my hearing's not as good as it was, so I've cut down on that kind of thing and only go occasionally to the House of Lords. The trouble is that if one's seen to be willing one can get caught up into a lifetime of such work, whereas a place like this alone is a full-time job in itself if it's to be run efficiently. Fortunately, I have a very good agent and staff and my elder son is increasingly interested in agriculture—very pleasant for me, of course, especially as we've recently acquired some farm land in New South Wales. One likes to think one is prepared to look ahead and tackle changing circumstances, as I said before. I think Australia has a wonderful future and I like to think my son might have some part to play in that future.'

Odd words perhaps from the sixth Earl of Bradford of its second creation, yet not so odd, perhaps, when it is remembered that a pertinacious and highly individual strain runs through this Bridgeman family, little known to the outside world, yet wholly wide-awake to the changing moods and manners of the frenetic twentieth century.

RAGLEY HALL

THE RAGLEY estate was bought in 1591 by the ambitious Conway family. The 1st Viscount considered rebuilding the existing house in the 1620s but it was left to the 3rd Viscount (later 1st Earl), onetime secretary of State to Charles II, to commission designs from Robert Hooke (1635-1703), a scholarly, cantankerous, ill-favoured Professor of Geometry at Gresham College, and colleague of Sir Christopher Wren. Hooke owed much to his study of French and Dutch architecture and these influences can be traced at Ragley.

Building was started in 1679. With its central block and four pavilions, the house was intended to be one of the most spectacular of its time. The project was probably over-ambitious for the family's finances, for, after Conway's death in 1683, the house remained empty until completed in the 1750s, and even after building had been restarted the house took many years to complete.

The next important development was carried out under the aegis of James Gibbs (1682-1754), who was primarily responsible for what is undoubtedly Ragley's most splendid architectural feature: the Great Hall, for which he designed, between 1750 and his death, the magnificent baroque decorations. Gibbs also seems to have been responsible for the design of the ceiling in the Study. There is also evidence to suggest that Francis Vassila, the stuccoist, was probably responsible for a certain amount of decorative work at Ragley in the middle years of the eighteenth century.

Later in the century James Wyatt added the impressive, if somewhat heavy, portico on the East Front and made alterations to the roof for Francis Ingram, the 2nd Marquess of Hertford, a close friend of the Prince Regent.

Opposite *Ragley Hall, seen from the West Front garden*

RAGLEY HALL lies twenty miles south of Birmingham, two miles outside Alcester on the A435. As is so often the case, the immediate countryside seems not particularly impressive, yet the landscape within the Ragley domain is undulating and beautiful. Those eighteenth-century patricians sited their houses with an eye for the country that wouldn't have disgraced a first-rate general in the field.

Lodges, curved stone walls and handsome iron gates open into a drive that takes the visitor past a cricket field, complete with pavilion, between casually maintained parkland towards the somewhat austerely symmetrical east front.

With its grey stone façade, fifteen bays wide, giant portico and undecorated pediment, set within a gravelled courtyard enclosed by rugged timber fencing, the house seems scarcely the home it turns out to be.

The house that the visitor sees now was designed by Robert Hooke, a contemporary of Christopher Wren and a notable architect (as well as scientist) who designed several other great houses, of which Ragley is the only one remaining. But the history of Ragley estate dates back to the eighth century when the estate belonged to Evesham Abbey. Much later it was sold to Sir John Rous who built an embattled castle. This lasted until 1680, by which time Ragley was already in the present owner's family, the Conways. The last of the Conways was created an Earl, and it was he who engaged Robert Hooke to design the new building in 1680, although it was many years before it was completed.

This architectural austerity of the exterior which first strikes the visitor is not noticeably diminished by the Great Hall, which is one of the most splendid yet awesome entrances to any of Britain's Stately Homes, almost a gargantuan double cube: seventy feet long, forty feet wide, forty feet high. Fortunately, this immense cubic space is enriched and enlivened by the decoration imposed by James Gibbs in the middle of the eighteenth century, a decorative scheme recently repainted in an audacious and wholly successful shade of pink.

Paired white Corinthian pilasters soar upwards to a cornice supporting a series of enormous shallow pointed-arch niches. These, in turn, sweep upwards to a ceiling with an immense centrepiece depicting Britannia, complete with a spear well clear of the ceiling.

The Hall furniture, decorated with the family coat of arms, was made for the Great Hall, five years after its completion. The cannon which command the extremely unmilitant approaches to Ragley were captured from a French man o' war in the early nineteenth century by Captain (later Admiral) Sir George Seymour, a nautical forebear of the present owner.

Hugh Edward Conway Seymour, the 8th Marquess of Hertford (created 1793); Baron Conway of Ragley (cr 1703); Baron Conway of Killultagh (1712); Earl of Hertford, Viscount Beauchamp (1750); Earl of Yarmouth (1793), makes no bones about his passion for Ragley.

'Frankly, I am emotional about the place,' he readily admits. 'I see no reason why I shouldn't be. It's one of the most beautiful houses in the country and it's mine. So why not?'

Rather more than most owners of Stately Homes, he is thoroughly justified in his passion, for the mere fact that Ragley stands at all is due solely to his own single-minded passion, resolution and imagination.

The story is rare in the post-war annals of the Stately Homes League, for this is the story of a house, already forsaken, which was rescued and given

The Marquess and Marchioness of Hertford

Opposite, above left and right *Two views of the Green Drawing-Room with Chinese Chippendale mirror and two eighteenth-century French commodes*

Below left *The Red Saloon; over the fireplace is Cornelius van Haarlem's painting 'The Raising of Lazarus'*

Below right *The Blue Drawing-Room with decorative ceiling by Wyatt*

fresh life in our own day.

Lord Hertford's father and uncle (from whom he inherited the title) died in the earliest days of the war whilst he was still at school. During the war Ragley became a hospital and inevitably took a great deal of punishment. Post-war, the family trustees decided that the house was already a white elephant of impossible proportions, and, with reluctance, doubtless tinged with relief, decided that the family should quit the house and move to the Home Farm. Meanwhile, the young man who had inherited the house was scarcely in the best strategic position to counter these plans, for by then he was a subaltern in the Grenadier Guards and was stationed in the Canal Zone.

But his ambition and determination to return to Ragley were as unyielding as his preparations for the task were practical. In 1953 he left the army, worked for a year as a farm labourer and then spent two years at Cirencester Agricultural College. In 1956 he left Cirencester, married Comtesse Louise de Camaran Chimay, daughter of Lt-Col Prince Alphonse de Chimay, and moved back into Ragley, setting about the immense task of making Ragley a place fit once more for Seymours to live in and others to visit.

Lord Hertford recalls these years with deceptively carefree phrases of unusual and engaging frankness. He is amongst the youngest of Stately Home owners, a youthful-looking thirty-eight: tall, fair-haired, clear-eyed, plainly endowed with considerable reserves of nervous and physical energy. He spends half the week at Ragley, the rest of the week in London where he is chairman of Hertford Public Relations, a fast-growing press and publicity organization with offices overlooking Fleet Street.

'Did your wife like the idea of moving back into Ragley?'

'Hated it. How could she do otherwise? A great place like that down on its uppers. And just the two of us. No staff. Nobody. That's literally true. My wife cooked. I helped around the place, getting in the firewood and so forth. I had to think twice about leaving my wife alone here when I had to stay away for a night on some business thing in London. That's why we got such an enormous dog.'

'Most people presumably thought you were off your head?'

'I saw their point. It *was* sheer madness judged by anybody's standards, especially those of my trustees, who included some practical hard-headed men of the world. They thought I was absolutely mad.'

'But now your wife says she hates leaving the place.'

'That's what Ragley does to one. Ensnares or enchants. Perhaps something of both. She comes up to London with me. Indeed, she likes our life in London almost as much as I do, but she can't wait to get back. But there it is. I share her views. To get back to Ragley at any time has been my major ambition. Now we're about half-way through our twenty-year programme for making Ragley the way it used to be. Little wonder I'm emotional about it.'

'But you'd be a lot better off if you were still living in the Home Farm?'

'I'd certainly be that, but one has to sort out one's own priorities, don't you think? Mine are simply my family, my house and my business. In that order. I quite enjoy the House of Lords when I go there, but it's not often. Of course keeping up Ragley, trying to restore it—despite generous government aid—costs me, personally, a hell of a lot of money.'

'But it's worth it?'

'For me it is. One can't tell for anybody else. One day my son may stand up and tell me if I hadn't spent so much on Ragley he might be a very rich fellow indeed. I'll have to wait a bit. At the moment he's ten so I've some time in hand. Meanwhile he and his three sisters love every

Opposite *Two views of the Library which looks out to the lake and Cotswold Hills beyond; above the chimneypiece is Reynold's portrait of Walpole*
Above *The South Staircase Hall*
Below *Gun captured at Tel-el-Kebir in 1882*

inch of the place. It's certainly a marvellous place for anyone to grow up in.'

'How do you account for your passion for the house?'

'Well, for one thing it's beautiful. For another, it was simply something I'd wanted to do from the time I was a schoolboy. From the time I inherited, in fact. I went into the army only for family reasons—after all, my father had commanded the Grenadiers. I also disliked living on the farm. I wanted to be here, at the heart of things. I wanted to look out *from* Ragley, not just *at* Ragley.'

'Did you like the army?'

'Hated it. I sometimes think that going to Cirencester was the first thing I ever did that gave me any real happiness. By that time I was twenty-four. That's a longish time to have to wait to start doing what one really wants to do.'

'But you've learned the knack.'

'I'd like to think so, but one can't always do all one wants to do all the time. For example, appearing on television, judging beauty competitions or taking part in panel games was very good for the tourist trade; but it is not so good for the middle-aged chairman of an industrially-minded public relations firm.'

'Regretfully?'

The Marquess nods. 'Fortunately, there's still a lot of scope for

Above *The Great Hall with its magnificent baroque decoration designed by James Gibbs in 1750. The ceiling centrepiece represents Britannia (detail below)*
Opposite *Nubian figures in the Great Hall*

enjoyment,' he adds.

'Do you enjoy running the estates as well as the house? Legend says your lands are fairly extensive.'

'We've eight thousand acres here. That's about twenty-five farms all told. I run four of them myself. That is, I have an absolutely first-class agent with whom I work very closely indeed. I try to spend Mondays looking after these matters. I quite enjoy them. My training at Cirencester stands me in good stead all the time.'

'Are you forester as well as farmer?'

'Up to a point. The woodlands at Ragley are our pride and joy. Timber for us is very much a crop. We've been working on what I'd call a profitable basis for two hundred years. We still are, thanks to my very able forestry manager. We supply every piece of timber needed for the farms, from fencing to cottage doors. We sell firewood to tenants. It's not one of Britain's major industries, but it helps.'

'Do you like working with British major industries in your Fleet Street life?'

'I thoroughly enjoy it. We touch industry—Swedish and British, oddly enough—at various points, from cross-channel ferries to a printing group, from motor cars to computers. I like the work and with my partners we seem to be making a success of the job.'

'How did you get into PR work?'

'Mainly because one of my closest friends, Bryan Thompson, a former national newspaper man, was already involved, together with Denys Hamilton, who had specialized for years in the industrial press, particularly mining and engineering. After a good deal of discussion we set up this business together. I like to think I've some kind of flair for the work, doubtless derived from the hard work I did getting Ragley put on the map inside ten years.'

'Now that Ragley is on the map, so to speak, do you mind seeing hundreds of people wandering round your place?'

'On the contrary, I desperately mind not having them. When we're open I like to see thousands of people wandering around. After all, a hundred people in the Great Hall are almost lost. And the park can give a thousand people a marvellous day out and still leave the place quite uncluttered.'

'You've no objections at all?'

'The only thing that does make me mad is when we've had the occasional party in the Great Hall and one sees visitors casually dropping their cigarette ends on to the carpet and actually grinding 'em in—just to make a thorough-going job. It may not be the most valuable carpet in the world but it's jolly useful and a pretty colour. That kind of thing can make my wife and myself very angry. Fortunately, it doesn't happen very often. Apart from that I delight in seeing people here. As I see it, I've got one of the most beautiful houses in England in my care. They seem to enjoy coming; so why not. It's a pity to keep these magnificent rooms all to oneself. I like seeing people enjoying the house. I like selling them guide-books.'

'Do you have guides as well?'

'Four ladies who know the history of the house answer visitors' questions. Occasionally we have a guided tour. But not very often. One can't please everybody. Some visitors want to be taken over the place step by step but most seem to like being left alone.'

'Do you label any of the paintings and so on?'

'Nothing. The relevant attributions are in the guide-book. It's far better to my mind that visitors should buy that and find out for them-

selves. It's all in the official guide—after all, I wrote it myself. Above all else, Ragley is a home and I want to keep it that way. Labels are OK in a museum but scarcely in a home.'

'How many visitors do you get?'

'On the average about fifty thousand a year.'

'Without gimmicks?'

'No gimmicks of any kind. How could I? As I said, this is my home. I live here. I think that's half the attraction for visitors. I know that some owners of large houses live elsewhere and drop in on their Stately Homes as if they were going to the office. *My* office is in London.'

'And you don't find an eighty-five-bedroomed house an unduly intimidating place to live in?'

'Certainly not nowadays. Four young children can make a house of this size quite a playground—and there are only about three rooms they aren't allowed to play in. And we have staff now. Only the barest minimum, I tell myself, but they're here. And a number of invaluable dailies. It's all a far cry from our first year here.'

'You don't mind the children romping about the place? Presumably the trampoline in the Great Hall belongs to them.'

'Yes, that belongs to them. I don't mind it there now the season's at an end. The only mishap we've had so far was when one of my daughters was chasing about in the Great Hall and brought down—and broke—one of those enormous nubian figures. I was so angry I'm afraid I overlooked the fact that she, poor dear, might have been hurt. But she wasn't—not a scratch. And Denis Wrey of Sloane Street made a splendid job of putting the figure to rights, so all ended happily. And such happenings help to teach one to keep possessions in perspective.'

'What kind of restoration work are you engaged in now?'

Opposite *The Dining-Room. The most splendid objects in this room are the four silver-gilt wine coolers made in the reign of George III. The plates are of silver and bear the family crest*
Above *The Prince Regent's Bedroom: the magnificent bed was specially made for the Prince Regent when he visited Ragley Hall*

'Well, it ranges from the most splendidly decorative to the most earthily utilitarian. On one hand we're redecorating the Study, the Library, the Green Drawing-Room and the State Bedroom—John Fowler's responsible for all that. At the other end of the scale we're installing new loo accommodation for visitors. After all, if people come here to spend a day in the park and the gardens, I feel that we should look after the practicalities of the situation. Up till now things have been mildly primitive, to say the least. Next year, I hope they're going to be well up to municipal standards.'

'Which is your favourite room?'

'We spend most of our lives in the Library, which inevitably makes it our favourite room: it's a perfect room for relaxing and working in. We've a notable library here, over thirty thousand books, of which ten thousand are in the Library. I like their companionship. And from my writing-table I can look across the lake to the Cotswolds beyond.'

'Any other favourite rooms?'

'Well, I like the Green Drawing-Room, too.'

'Do you ever speak on the Stately Homes in the House of Lords?'

'So far I haven't, although it's my favourite subject—at least Ragley is. If I'm asked to give a lecture I just say I've only got one subject—Ragley—take it or leave it. My particular subject in the House of Lords is prison reform and the after-care of prisoners. I'm a member of The New Bridge which sets out to help ex-prisoners.'

A curious cause, some might think for the ex-army owner of a vast estate still held by his family after nearly three centures, but, in this case, the cause seems eminently logical and natural for this warm-hearted, lively-minded landowner-farmer-businessman who says people come first and seems to practise his theories first-hand.

HAREWOOD HOUSE

HENRY LASCELLES, a Yorkshire squire, bought the old mansion of Gawthorpe in 1738, but it was his son, Edwin, who decided to demolish the mansion and to build afresh. To this end he commissioned John Carr of York to design the new Harewood House, after rejecting designs by Sir William Chambers, who had been working on various projects at Harewood including the stables. Carr had worked under Chambers on the stables and he had begun to build that model village sponsored by Lascelles which is now separated from the entrance to Harewood House by the Leeds-Harrogate road. Presumably Lascelles found working with the local man more congenial than working with the somewhat magisterial metropolitan master.

Carr began to build, but, following a visit by Robert Adam in connexion with the restoration of Harewood Church, (an ancient foundation, dating back to 1116), he, in turn, seems to have been ousted as architect, although he continued to build the house for Lascelles. There is now no means of deciding which parts of the house were designed by which architect, although Adam was undoubtedly responsible for the whole of the interior decoration, for which he used the talents of Rose and Collins for the plasterwork, Angelica Kaufmann, Antonio Zucchi and Biagio Rebecca for decorative paintings, and also commissioned furniture from Thomas Chippendale.

Collaterally with the building of his new house, Edwin Lascelles also set about the task of replanning and replanting the surrounding countryside. His own gardener, Sparrow, began the project by damming a stream to make the lake. In 1772 Capability Brown was called in to advise. During the following decade he evolved one of his most notable naturalistic landscape gardens, which his biographer* has justly termed "one of the most delectable of landscapes".

The house remained much as Carr and Adam had designed it for over seventy years, but, in 1843, the wife of the 3rd Earl, finding the house too incommodious for her ideas of entertaining, called in Sir Charles Barry, designer of the Houses of Parliament, to provide plans which would give the house more bedrooms. In the ensuing aggrandisement of the house, Barry added an extra storey and did away with the portico on the front. The handsome four-square simplicity of the Carr-Adam house was thus overlaid by what was virtually a transplanted Italian palazzo. This new *ambiente* was underlined by the introduction of vast terraces and fountains set above the formal gardens—scarcely the ideal accompaniment to Brown's essay in The Picturesque. Yet the magnificent landscaped gardens were to suffer an even more desperate blow a century later when 20,000 trees were uprooted in a disastrous storm in February 1962. Replanting was started at once and continues to revive the 'delectable landscape'.

Today, the family have taken over the top floor of the house, leaving the major part of Harewood House available for the display of its incomparable decorations and furniture.

Opposite *The South Front of Harewood House seen from the park*

* *Capability Brown* by Dorothy Stroud (Country Life)

LORD HAREWOOD maintains three highly disparate interests in easy equilibrium: his home, music and football. All three also happen to be professional interests, for none nowadays can sustain, or be sustained by, the strictly amateur approach.

In order to survive as a home and as something a good deal more than a museum, a Stately Home now needs careful and expert supervision over a number of interests, from forestry and farming, to accountancy and the law. For the gifted amateur, music can still prove as intense a pleasure as it always has been, of course, but Lord Harewood has sought out the more adventurous and demanding spheres of the professional music world and shown himself to be eminently at home amongst its masters. And, as every schoolboy knows, professional football is what football, ultimately, is all about. Lord Harewood, an enthusiastic player of the game as a youth, has, for several years, been President of Leeds United Football Club, champions of the English Football League and successful participants in the tougher realms of European competition.

George Henry Hubert Lascelles, 7th Earl of Harewood, got to know Harewood quite early in life: he remembers visiting his grandparents there when he was three or four, and he began to live there when he was seven soon after his father inherited.

'I enjoyed my boyhood here,' he says. 'It was a wonderful place in which to grow up. My parents ran it with some degree of grandeur, I suppose. Certainly judged by present-day standards. Unlike many houses of this size, even in those days of abundant staff—especially in Yorkshire—the place was never cold on even the coldest days. Wood and coal fires burned throughout the house. There was always somebody to bring more. Alfred Blades, my butler, remembers an indoor staff of twenty-seven and house parties with forty for dinner in the big Dining Room and nine serving at table, and gold or silver services in use. Things are a good deal different now, as you might imagine, but Blades is still here. Life is no less interesting and rewarding. The gold and silver plate has been sold, but I shed few tears. The fact is I love it here and resent being away.'

'How much time can you spend here?'

'Something like half the year and it's gradually getting longer. This is apt to surprise some of my friends but it's true.'

'But you still maintain a lot of musical interests in London.'

'True, but a lot can be done over the telephone and we're only six miles from one end of the Motorway here and six miles from the beginning of the M1 in London. We usually drive. It's cheaper and basically faster, without ever exceeding motorway legal limits.'

Lady Harewood, an Australian by birth, echoes these views. 'I'd always lived an urban life. I wondered how I'd settle down in the West Riding. Now I feel the same way. I love it here. I love the house and the marvellous outlook. One needs London for recharging one's batteries and so forth. I suppose our ideal arrangement is to have the best of both worlds—London and Yorkshire—and I suspect we've got it, but once I'm up here I long to stay here—week after week.'

'Did you know the house before?'

'Not before I came to live here—until after we were married. I'd known of Harewood, of course, but only by picture and legend. When I came here to live—with some degree of apprehension—I loved it from the very first moment and I get more and more involved in the house and gardens and farms year by year.'

The Earl and Countess of Harewood
Opposite *The spectacular Entrance Hall has a stone floor and dark porphyry marble red ceiling decorations and pilasters. The Adamesque elbow chairs have circular carved wooden backs bearing the Harewood crest*

Above *The Spanish Library. The wall covering between the Adam ceiling and Victorian bookcases is of seventeenth-century Spanish leather. The painting, seen on the left, is 'St John the Baptist' by Ribera*
Opposite *The Library with its beautifully colourful ceiling and light mahogany Victorian bookcases added by the architect, Sir Charles Barry, in 1845*

The Harewoods live on the top floor of the house in what were once the bedrooms of friendly visitors and relatives. (Not the really grand visitors: they were always placed in the north-facing rooms, presumably because Harewood, in common with most other English Palladian houses, was slavishly copied from Italian prototypes in which the northern rooms offered the coolest conditions for favoured visitors—as they do in England, of course, with less felicitous results.) Thus the Harewoods' commodious sitting-room, an erstwhile bedroom sited above the library, has none of the ceiling and cornice decoration of the more stately nearby north bedroom. What it does have, however, is one of the most splendid and unspoiled outlooks in northern England, overlooking Capability Brown's landscaped lakes and woodlands rising to the high ridge of the dales which make the rugged and impressive horizons of Harewood.

This view is seen through most unusual windows: large but square six-pane windows, inset scarcely above the high skirting. These windows seem to frame the outside panoramas in far stranger and more exciting patterns than more conventionally shaped elongated windows. Anyone sitting in a chair or sofa facing the window sees not just sky as might be expected from this high vantage point, but the dales. It is a surprising upending of the

A Chippendale commode inlaid with ivory and an Adam mirror in the Princess Royal's Sitting Room
Opposite *The Gallery, 76 feet long, has wooden pelmets carved to resemble heavy blue taffeta. Four decorative oval paintings by Angelica Kaufmann surmount the tall mirrors between the windows. The ceiling is by Adam*

normal outlook. The Harewoods thus have the best of both worlds in their house, too, for their rooms are of comfortable size, warm and colourful and pleasantly furnished with a selection from the less spectacular pieces for which Harewood is renowned amongst students of the history of English furniture.

Harewood stands high in the midst of its domain of dales, darkly impressive, particularly on a low-clouded day, with its sombre stonework and pilastered façades.

The house, adjacent to the village of Harewood in the West Riding of Yorkshire, is approached via a drive which opens between two lodges which have a stern, keep-out quality about them.

But all this seeming remoteness and reticence is belied by the interior of the house, especially by the entrance hall, an enormous stone-floored room, which has been restored and redecorated during the past year with spectacular results.

'It was a problem room and nearly drove us mad,' Lord Harewood frankly confesses. 'We wanted colour but it was no good getting garish. And this is really the only room here which remains much as Carr of York designed it for my forebear, Edwin Lascelles, in seventeen fifty nine. As you may know, he was well on the way with the house when he was joined by the young Robert Adam, still in his twenties but rising fast as the fashionable new architect. Yet Carr never seems to have been unduly tetchy about the change, even though his mother was a Lascelles. Obviously we wanted the hall to be a fitting introduction to the house, but not a decorator's day out. Richard Buckle, a great friend, who has a remarkable eye and flair in these matters, was of tremendous help and finally we settled on this colour scheme of pale grey walls, the niches in white, and the deep dark porphyry marble red for the ceiling decorations and the pilasters. *We* think it works very well and other people seem to agree.'

Certainly no other entrance to any great house has spanned the centuries in so spectacular a manner. The room would not have been this way in the eighteenth century and it would not be this way had those great decorators of the eighteenth never lived. It is all that such an entrance should be: scenic, dramatic, heroic, like a set for the opening of some magnificent opera by Berlioz. That Mr Buckle, designer of spectacularly successful pageants, exhibitions and spectacles, had a hand in this *tour de force*, comes as no surprise.

One of the major triumphs in this scheme of redecoration attends one of the minor elements: the hall chairs. These, the most Adamesque chairs in a house unusually well-endowed with beautiful chairs, are decorative elbow chairs with circular carved wooden backs. They have now been stripped of their Victorian varnish and repainted in pale grey and white, with the Harewood crest picked out in bright colours in the centre of the circular backs.

Lord Harewood leads the way from this spectacular entrance hall through the State Rooms of his house with lively enthusiasm, his knowledgeable but light-hearted discourse taking in decoration, paintings, furniture and *objets d'art*. His asides add to the humanity of the great house:

(In the Old Library) 'This room was just long enough for my father and my aunt to play cricket in.'

(In his father's sitting room) 'Some dealers at the Harrogate Antiques Fair were raving about this pair of mahogany commodes. I like them, but I prefer some of the other Chippendale pieces. They are a pair, of course . . . '

(In the China Room) 'I've a particular fondness for the French service in this cabinet with its miscellany of transfer views of French churches and English Country houses. A curious mixture by any standards. Notre Dame, Le Chateau de Holkham, Le Chateau de Harewood. The Room was designed by Adam, as Mr Lascelles' dressing-room, but I decided to convert into this china room ten years ago . . . '

(In the Library) 'One of my favourite pieces of contrast in this house full of contrasts is here: between Barry's mahogany bookcases and Adam's infinitely lighter—and gayer—touch in the ceilings. But they seem to live together very amicably, probably due to the marvellous shade of the mahogany, don't you think?'

And so on.

Inevitably, because Lord Harewood's mother was Princess Royal, many visitors, with that inveterate interest in the Royal Family which seems to dominate the minds of tourists, whether native or foreign, are deeply preoccupied with family paintings and photographs. These are to be seen in the Princess Royal's Sitting Room, rather than the Dressing Room, converted by Sir Herbert Baker in 1929 in a kind of neo-Adam style with plaster decorations by Sir Charles Wheeler PPRA. Both this room, with its semi-domed ceiling, and her husband's sitting-room, with its pictures by Sir Alfred Munnings, Sir John Lavery and Frank Salisbury, evoke that recent, but utterly departed, between-the-wars era with the vividness of a play by Noel Coward or a novel by Evelyn Waugh.

Yet it is to the magnificent Chippendale furniture that the visitor to Harewood returns: to those pieces, presumably designed by Adam and certainly made by Chippendale in his workshop in St Martin's Lane, for many of the bills are still preserved in the house. A secretaire and two commodes in the Princess Royal's Sitting Room are renowned throughout the specialist world of furniture historians. One of the commodes, inlaid with ivory, cost £86 in 1773. Now a thousand times that sum might not buy such a piece in the sale-rooms.

This room also contains a remarkable collection of water-colours of Harewood, including several by Thomas Malton, showing Harewood as it appeared before the great changes wrought by the joint efforts of the wife of the 3rd Earl and Sir Charles Barry, architect of the Houses of Parliament. The Countess, needing more bedrooms and perhaps a more splendid façade, brought in Barry to carry out her schemes of aggrandisement. They succeeded only too well. In the transition, the foursquare, sturdy, handsome simplicity of Carr's design was swept away. Anyone examining the paintings by Girtin, Varley and Malton cannot help but sympathize with the present owner's lament that these alterations were ever carried out. 'The house as Carr and Adam planned it would have been so very much more suitable for twentieth-century living,' says the present owner. Apart from which, twentieth-century architectural enthusiasts are apt to be more appreciative of the simplicities of Carr than the intricacies of Barry.

Lord Harewood's interest in music has taken a highly practical and adventurous form in his own house. A series of concerts was given last year (ranging from Boris Christoff singing Russian songs to George Malcolm playing the harpsichord, with the Janacek String Quartet and many others in between) and another will be given this year (covering as wide a field; from Ravi Shankar to Schoenberg). The recitals take place in the Gallery, a room almost eighty feet long, and over twenty in height and width. This room is chiefly renowned—again amongst specialists—for its pelmets, carved and painted in Chippendale's workshop to simulate heavy blue taffeta. These were the only curtains Adam wished this room

The East Bedroom with its fourposter bed designed by Adam
Opposite *The formal gardens on the South Front overlooking Capability Brown's beautiful naturalistic landscape gardens*

to have, but blue side curtains were added in Victorian times. 'When my great grandmother—Queen Alexandra—came here on a visit,' Lord Harewood says *en passant*, 'she called for a long stick and insisted on tapping the pelmets to prove to herself they really were wood. Other visitors have to take 'em on trust.'

The Gallery can seat about 200 people for one of the Harewoods' concerts, and the acoustics make the gallery a perfect background for such musical occasions, with listeners able to indulge visual as well as aural faculties with the sight of the William Kent console, the Angelica Kaufmann cartouches above the great pier-glasses and the magnificent ceiling designed by Adam and carried out by Joseph Rose.

Seven thousand acres of Wharfedale encompass Harewood, reduced by death duties after the early death of the 6th Earl from the 20,000 that he had inherited.

The reduced estate is intensively developed: over twenty farms, accounting for half the acreage, are let to tenants, and the Home Farm of over 1,400 acres (of which 600 acres are devoted to corn production) supports a dairy herd, beef herd, four hundred ewes and over a thousand pigs. Another thousand acres are woodland under a head forester and staff of ten. Four hundred acres have been planted since the last war. The timber produced and marketed is of high quality, mainly sycamore, oak and beech, and the estate sawmill is run on a sufficiently commercial basis to require a good deal of outside timber for conversion and sale. Even the pleasure grounds make their contribution to this enterprise: Harewood roses are sent all over England and abroad.

Here is one Stately Home that accepts to the full the implications of the century.

TYNINGHAME CASTLE

THE TWO HOMES of the Haddingtons could scarcely be more different: Tyninghame a typical 'Scottish domestic' house near Dunbar, which was enlarged, decorated and generally transformed and aggrandized in the Regency era, and Mellerstain, near Kelso, a great Adam Stately Home, castellated and austere.

George Baillie, whose Mellerstain estate had been made forfeit after he had been in desperate conflict with the English government in the 1680s, fled to Holland and became one of William of Orange's closest attendants. On William's accession to the English throne in 1689, Baillie returned with him. His estate was restored; he became an M.P. and one of the leading protagonists for the Treaty of Union (1706-7).

But these things took time and the new house was not begun until 1725, when William Adam was asked to prepare plans for a new house. But only the two flanking wings were built and thus they remained for over forty years, probably due to the fact that Baillie died in 1738. His younger daughter married Lord Binning, son of the Earl of Haddington, but it was his grandson, who assumed the name of Baillie, who was responsible for the completion of the Mellerstain we see today.

The house, which has now passed into the ownership of Lord Binning, the Earl of Haddington's son, was built near the old house of which only a vaulted ruin—known as the Boyle House and reputedly haunted—now remains.

The sponsor of this resuscitation, George Baillie, had travelled widely in Europe and was impressed—as were most of the aristocracy of the time—by the ideas of Robert Adam (1728-92), son of the builder of the still-standing wings. He commissioned Robert Adam to complete the house.

Adam linked the two wings in a simple unostentatious manner, leaving the interior for the full display of his architectural and decorative genius. The library and dining-room are amongst Adam's finest achievements. Unfortunately, his designs (which still exist) for the ceiling of the Great Gallery were never carried out. The house has remained virtually unaltered since that, although Sir Reginald Blomfield (1856-1942), the eminent Edwardian architect, was commissioned to transform the grounds which slope from the house to the lake into a series of terraces in the grand manner of the time.

Tyninghame is a far less Stately Home, being an adaptation of a smaller 'Scottish domestic' house of some antiquity, possibly deriving from a much earlier house built to withstand chance attack. Certainly there has long been a house of some kind at Tyninghame. Its present pinnacled-red-sandstone aspect, however, dates from the alterations sponsored by the 9th Earl. He, in 1830, commissioned a scheme for giving the house a somewhat grander interior and more impressive exterior from William Burn (1789-1870) an Edinburgh architect who later established a very successful London practice.

Opposite *A view of Lady Haddington's private sitting room*

Above *The 60-foot long Drawing-Room with its original fitted carped carpet dating from 1830*
Below left *The Ante Drawing-Room, between the Library and the Drawing-Room, houses family portraits by Jamesone, Raeburn and Reynolds*
Right *The formal Dining-Room with its series of portraits of the Stuarts, to whom the Haddingtons swore an oath of allegiance*
Opposite *A corner of the Drawing-Room showing the portrait of Isabelle d'Este by Jules Romains*

BERLIN

GEORGE BAILLIE-HAMILTON, 12th Earl of Haddington, is quick to emphasize that the families of Baillie *and* Hamilton are dual elements in his lineage, and, to this fact, owes (or owed) possession two of the most splendid houses in Scotland: Mellerstain and Tyninghame. Mellerstain is now in the possession of his son, but the two East Lothian houses remain a linked thread in the family life of the Haddingtons.

Mellerstain is, of course, one of the legendary houses of Britain: a castellated Adam house, with an extraordinary break in its building history. The two wings, begun in 1725, were built first—by William Adam for George Baillie of Jerviswood—but no mansion was built for almost half a century. The wings continued to flank what was presumably the older house or an empty space. Then, in about 1770, William Adam's son, Robert, by then the most influential architect and arbiter of taste in Britain, completed the house for his grandson, also George Baillie.

The present Earl of Haddington lived at Mellerstain for over thirty years, and then moved fifty miles north to Tyninghame.

'How could you bear to uproot yourself from that beautiful house after spending almost half your life there?'

'My mother, Lady Binning, could have lived at Mellerstain, but she preferred to live at Tyninghame. When she died in 1952, my wife and I moved to Tyninghame.'

'And never regretted it?'

'Not really. I love Mellerstain—as does my wife. One can't live in a handsome historic house for almost half one's life without its atmosphere taking hold of one. But there it is. We left Mellerstain and we've now been at Tyninghame for some twelve years. And enjoyed every minute of it.'

'You don't find the architectural differences between the two houses give you any sense of nostalgia for Mellerstain?'

'Well, obviously Tyninghame can't be compared with Mellerstain architecturally, but it has its own Scottish style and quality.'

'Presumably you also have more land here?'

'No, not so much. We've about seven thousand acres here—we go right down to the North Sea—with eight farms and a good deal of forest land. Looking after that, even with the help of a very efficient agent, takes a fair amount of time. Then I have the other kinds of interests. I'm fond of books, reading and writing, and I'm President of the Royal Company of Archers, Trustee of the National Library, President of the A.P.R.S. I was also President of the Scottish Georgian Society, and past-President of the Society of Antiquaries and so on.'

'Do you have any commercial interests?'

'Not in a city sense. We run the woodlands here on a commercial basis with our own saw-mills and so on, but I've never been involved in industry. I was in the army, in the First War. Afterwards I was ADC to the Governor General in Canada—where I met my wife. Then I came back to Mellerstain and took up civilian life for the first time. In the last war I was in the army

Opposite *Views of the gardens at Tyninghame;* top left, *a fountain where the axes of the formal garden cross;* right, *Orpheus in stone;* below, *the eighteenth-century-seeming gazebo, sheltering Flora from the breezes of the Forth, is, in fact, only two years old*
Above *The North Front of Mellerstain with the William Adam wing*

again—in tanks as the cavalry had become by then, but, oddly enough, at forty-five I found myself in the Air Force.'

'And then you returned to civilian life again?'

'Ever since the end of the war I've always found there's plenty to do up here. I'm Lord Lieutenant for the County of Berwickshire, and although this isn't the most demanding county in Britain, it does mean that I can often help in County affairs. It's mostly farming country, of course, but as that's a major interest of my own I've always enjoyed the job. Then for several years I was one of the sixteen hereditary peers permitted by statute to sit in the House of Lords. Now any Scottish peer is entitled to attend and speak if he feels like speaking.'

'What were your subjects?'

'I used to speak on Scottish affairs, the Arts and forestry in particular, but I don't do so much now. In fact, I doubt whether I'm in London for more than forty days a year. I love Scotland, and I'm very much a countryman. My life is here, looking after my lands in what I suppose would be called the traditional manner. I enjoyed riding and hunting for many years—race riding in particular. My life's been spent almost wholly in Scotland, and for the last twelve years, as I said, here.'

'Could we return to the subject of your move from Mellerstain, for a moment? Tyninghame must have been a curious experience after the eighteenth-century atmosphere of Mellerstain?'

'They are very different, of course. The present house at Tyninghame is Regency, and is an adaptation of the smaller "Scottish domestic" house. There's always been some sort of house there, but my forebear, the 9th Earl, a politician and a close friend of Canning's, undoubtedly wanted a grander place and, in 1830, commissioned William Burn to alter it."

'Presumably the red sandstone pinnacled turrets were part of his transformation.'

'I imagine so. The sandstone was probably built over the original stone structure, which was probably coated with roughcast—what we call "harled" in Scotland. We're apt to regard roughcast with somewhat greater favour than the English. Whatever it was—and we've only got a small pencil and ink drawing of 1780 to go by—it was probably the usual Scottish castle-form—basically a modest kind of fortress-cum-residence with the emphasis on ruggedness and so forth. Then the castle got the red stone treatment and what were then doubtless considered far more sophisticated elevations. Briefly, more windows and those pinnacled turrets.'

'Very different elevations from Mellerstain's.'

'Very. Personally, I prefer Mellerstain's, of course, and I'm always glad to have that beautiful painting of the house by Felix Kelly at Tyninghame, which shows Mellerstain from across the lake that Sir Reginald Blomfield designed to supplant one that my forebear George Baillie put in long ago in the form of a Dutch canal—doubtless to remind him of the land which had offered him refuge when he fled to the continent during the troubles of the "Revolution" in Scotland.'

'You seem to have done marvels with the gardens at Tyninghame.'

'That's all my wife's work. You published a feature on the gardens in your magazine. I rather agree with what your gardening editor wrote—that it's the work of a remarkably accomplished—and modest—gardener and garden-planner. As you know, there are two main gardens here: the old walled garden a quarter of a mile away—that's in the old Scottish style, and the pleasure grounds surrounding the house. My wife works on one primary principle which I think ought to be more widely followed by gardeners in seeking to keep as much as possible of the original garden that's taken over. So many gardeners seem to want to tear up all that their

predecessors have done, but my wife contends that it can't all be wrong. I think my wife's done marvels here—as the French *Amateurs de Jardins* who came here *en masse* last summer, seemed to agree.'

'You seem to be able to grow roses well up here.'

'My wife takes a particular pleasure in old roses such as the gallicas, bourbons and damasks, which we also grow in abundance at Mellerstain.'

'Are you a gardener yourself?'

'I spend a lot of time in the garden, but my main interest is forestry. Now that I'm in my seventies I seem to be taking extra pleasure in planting some of the exotic trees which aren't supposed to be all that hardy in Scotland. Eucalyptus, for example. I find we can grow the Gunnii species fairly confidently. Nevertheless, I go on experimenting. I find when one is older planting trees for posterity a most satisfactory pastime.'

'Apart from gardening your wife also seems to have a rare talent for interior decoration.'

'That's very true. Another reason why I like the house so much.'

The interior of Tyninghame contains one of the most unexpected assemblies of rare and handsome furniture (much of it French) to be found in any house in Britain. The furniture includes several enriched *bombé* commodes of exceptional splendour. These pieces are incorporated in decorative themes that, for colour, ingenuity and imaginative quality, would put most professional decorators' schemes to shame. Lady Haddington's interiors are enchanting exercises in originality and authority. She uses colour with the mastery of an artist and matches that rarest of talents with an eye for contrasting textures and patterns. No Stately Home has been enlivened so gaily and unpompously with such a series of pleasurable rooms.

The family dining room, opening on to the garden and facing a magnificent ilex, is a low-ceilinged room with a large circular table and chairs set against an unusual wall-covering. This consists of panels of minute red-and-white check chintz traditionally used to line Victorian and Edwardian curtains which have been pleated and mounted on battens. The resulting panels are framed in plain red chintz. The total effect is enchanting.

Lady Haddington's own sitting room, also overlooking the garden, is a small, gaily-coloured comfortable room with a magnificent French writing-table set at right-angles to the window, overlooking the gardens she has transformed during the past dozen years.

The library has become the family sitting-room and the background of leather-bound volumes and another magnificent *bombé* chest, combined with deep sofas, makes this room a far cry from all legends of the daunting chills of Scotland's baronial halls.

For the unusual patterns and qualities of her fabrics, Lady Haddington gives full marks to John Fowler; the most sympathetic of decorators. 'He never tries to impose his will on a client as so many decorators try to do,' she says. 'He's a scholar as well as a decorator. He's quite unique in my experience.'

The interiors at Tyninghame are both splendid yet domestic. Those at Mellerstain splendid yet formal, an inevitable fact when it is remembered that the library ceiling at Mellerstain is generally reckoned to be one of the masterpieces of Robert Adam's particular form or decoration, with a circular oil painting of Minerva flanked by representations of teaching and learning, all probably by Zucchi. Added to this is the remarkable series of panels above the bookcases, each depicting a scene from the legends of Ancient Greece. But for Lord and Lady Haddington the simpler pleasures of Tyninghame suffice—a view likely to be echoed by any visitor fortunate enough to have visited both homes of the Haddingtons.

Opposite *The Mellerstain Library is entirely Adam; the ceiling, dated 1770 and resembling a piece of Wedgewood stoneware, is considered to be one of his masterpieces*

SHUGBOROUGH

PRIOR TO the Reformation, Shugborough was in the possession of the Bishops of Lichfield, but afterwards passed into secular ownership, finally coming into the Anson family in 1642.

The estate passed from William Anson (d. 1644), a Staffordshire lawyer with a successful London practice, to a grandson who built a three-storied brick house in 1693.

That house forms the central block of the present house, built by Thomas Anson, brother of the Admiral, Lord Anson, famous as a naval warrior, administrator and reformer. The admiral had made himself a rich man as a result of prize money gained by his attacks upon the Spanish South American fleet. Marrying late in life and dying in 1762, without an heir, he bequested both Shugborough and his fortune to his elder brother Thomas, a man of unusually wide interest, artistic, industrial and political. Thomas Anson commissioned his friend, the architect James ('Athenian') Stuart, designer of Anson's London house, to design the monuments, *inter alia* to Admiral Anson, which still adorn the park. Stuart also carried out various alterations to the house and supervised the decoration of some rooms.

Yet it was Thomas Anson's grandson, Thomas William Anson (1767-1818) who was responsible for the transformation of Shugborough. Between 1790 and 1806 he commissioned Samuel Wyatt to enlarge and remodel the house. He also greatly extended the park, removed the local village, and even diverted the Stafford-Lichfield road to suit his purpose.

Wyatt gave the house its most notable feature: the Ionic portico which adorns the central block of the entrance front. The columns are unusually constructed of slate, very ingeniously worked to give a fluted effect. Wyatt also encased the whole house with slates, simulated to give the effect of stonework. He also used the discarded balustrade surmounting the three-storied block as a linking device with the flanking two-storey wings. The general effect of these thoughtful changes was to give the long eastern elevation a unity which it had certainly never previously possessed and to reduce the apparent dominance of the central block.

During the first years of the nineteenth century Wyatt also designed a central three-storey feature on the west front, which was, unfortunately, vastly enlarged almost half-a-century ago, thus destroying Wyatt's carefully considered western elevation. Further alterations were made to the house during the 1920s, not all enhancing its symmetry and splendour. Thus Wyatt's great bow on the western front was remodelled with over-emphatic results to the elevation, the encasing slates were removed and the exterior stuccoed. Nevertheless, on the east front the visitor sees the house that Wyatt so skilfully and sympathetically rebuilt.

Opposite *The Bird Room, with Wyatt's decorative ceiling and Aubusson carpet*

Lord Lichfield in his London home
Opposite, top left *Lord Lichfield's bedroom has khaki-coloured walls, white ceiling and dado; curtaining and bedcover are in shades of pink and orange*
Right *The circular Regency breakfast room, decorated with striped wallpaper and sepia prints*
Bottom left *Lord Lichfield's private study*
Right *Turquoise and emerald-green patterned walls match the bed-hangings in one of the bedrooms*

THE MAIN approach to Shugborough fulfils all those criteria demanded by theorists of the picturesque. A pair of small, square, handsome lodges, just off the main Stafford-Lichfield road, introduces the visitor to a mile-long drive of almost medieval wildness: great trees on either side with innumerable rhododendron bushes for summer relief with an untamed landscape beyond. Then, suddenly, wildness ends and the vista opens on to wide, undulating parkland, majestic specimen trees and the architectural follies made possible by the prize money won by an Admiral of the Fleet.

The house is low-lying, its dominant feature an immense colonnaded portico along the central bays of the entrance front flanked by two wings with circular pepperpot features at their farthest limits.

Within the nearer of these wings—the western end of the house—the Earl of Lichfield has made his Shugborough home.

Thomas Patrick John Anson, 5th Earl of Lichfield, 6th Viscount Anson, 6th Baron Soberton, is just thirty. He has been the object of considerable newspaper publicity inevitably likely to attend the somewhat *mouvmenté* career of a youngish ex-guardee nobleman with good looks, long (but well-tended) hair, far-from-guardee (but well-tended) moustache and a most fastidious but highly individual taste in clothes, emphatically not in the Savile Row mode. But he is plainly made of durable stuff, takes the newspaper comment as it comes and makes no bones about the fact that he enjoys life, enjoys being a photographer, enjoys being a Lord and will continue in his enjoyments despite the less agreeable inquisitiveness of gossip columnists and their kin.

That he is made of durable material is well shown by the way he has coped with a situation that would have brought many another scion to his patrician knees, for he has probably taken greater financial punishment as a result of Britain's death duties and probate laws than anyone of his time, apart, perhaps, from the Duke of Devonshire.

The story is quirky and mildly macabre. In the early nineteen-fifties, his grandfather, the 4th Earl of Lichfield, made over the Shugborough estates of some 9,000 acres to Lord Lichfield's father. This seemed at the time a reasonable and judicious procedure, for his grandfather was then in his seventies and his father in his forties. Not so. In 1958, soon after the five-year clearance period (by which time the gift was legally absolute) his father died of a heart attack and his grandfather (perhaps of despair) two years later. This tragedy was further clouded by the fact that his father, who had parted from his mother ten years earlier, had remarried only three months before his death. Thus, within two years, the estate had suffered two lots of enormous death duties.

The Probate Office, more concerned with legalities than sentiment, pressed on, gathering in the shekels by selling Shugborough's treasures. Lord Lichfield's coming-of-age was more a dirge than a celebration. Two years previously, any bookmaker would have given certain odds that Patrick Anson would one day be an earl *and* a millionaire. By 1960 he was certainly one but very emphatically not the other.

At the time he was a subaltern in the Grenadier Guards. 'I don't recall that my enjoyment of life was greatly diminished,' he says, 'although I knew it was a situation I'd have to face sooner or later—with the help of my trustees.'

'And what did happen?'

'Thanks largely to the efforts of my step-mother, who stayed on for three years after my grandfather's death, Shugborough was handed over to the

National Trust with a sizable endowment—but only after the roof had been restored and reslated to the high specifications demanded by the Trust. Very rightly they'll only take over a building with a sound roof,' Lord Lichfield explains as he paces along the river that runs to the north of the house. 'No matter how historical and architecturally interesting the house, the roof's got to be O.K. Reroofing Shugborough cost the best part of fifty thousand pounds. Now it seems to be in pretty good order for years to come. Apart from that, the Trust needed an endowment of ten thousand a year for the upkeep of the house before they were prepared to take it on. As you see, it's not just a simple matter of handing over a Stately Home and then sitting back. But my step-mother did a fine job. She probably loved Shugborough more than any of the rest of the family. In fact, only because of her diligent sorting-out were the papers and documents, now in the care of the National Trust and county archivist, preserved. After I moved in she went to live in Cornwall. I owe her a great deal.'

By twists of circumstance Lord Lichfield has already enjoyed two careers of the utmost disparity, and, most curious experience of all, perhaps, lived through a completely Victorian childhood in the nineteen-forties.

He grew up at Shugborough, surrounded by the trappings, protocol and zaniness that great wealth and the country life of the English upper crust were apt to sponsor in earlier times. The major influences in the young Anson's life was his grandfather, the 4th Earl, then in his seventies, but still a larger-than-life-size personality and a man of unusual vigour. Until the Second World War this feudally minded martinet maintained an indoor staff of thirty and up to twenty gardeners, ruling them all with the same despotic detachment that he exercised over son and grandson.

His son, the heir-apparent, escaped to the Second World War, but the grandson, born in 1939, lived apprehensively (yet, in a curious way, appreciatively) within the shadow of his grandfather's seeming omnipotence. He now remembers his grandfather's oddities with relish, but it is easy to share his erstwhile fears. The Earl believed in toughening-up the young, starting as early as possible. 'My room was in the outside tower so that it was the coldest room in the house—and the smallest. So I also had the narrowest bed. Some winters the ink in the inkwells froze. I wasn't allowed any kind of hot-water bottle until I was about five and then it was one of those earthenware jobs I could scarcely carry and which bruised one's toes when one turned in the night.'

'What did your parents say?'

'Oh, my father agreed. It was the way he'd been brought up.'

'And your mother?'

'Well, she wasn't exactly enamoured of the system, but, like myself, she conformed.'

'Did you ever join forces? Your grandfather sounds fairly fearsome.'

'He wasn't actually. He was something of a despot, but nothing of a tyrant, but, inevitably, with my father at the wars, my mother and myself became very close. We've remained close ever since. I have only the happiest memories of her at Shugborough, although she wasn't there, of course, for a great deal of my childhood. After she and my father parted she moved to London. Later, happily, she remarried. But I well remember opening the doors of the State Rooms one by one from one end of the house when my mother was playing the piano—she had been a concert pianist—and gradually walking towards the Music Room so that the volume increased door by door as if I were controlling it—like a conductor.'

'Your grandfather seems a carry-over from another age.'

'I think so. Some of his actions were inexplicable. He even communicated with his butler by the written word, although they were in the same room a score of times a day. We have hundreds of these *aides memoires* in a cupboard here. *The whiting had too many bones*, for instance. Too bad, of course, but it was a bit late in the day for a note to say so. And the last one of all, very much to the point: 'Beans cold. Butler farted'. And I well remember the first time I was finally allowed to eat with him and the family in the dining-room—I had had meals in my nursery until I was seven, and then in the servants' dining-hall until I was fourteen. He asked me to bring his vintage port from the sideboard. As the only drink I'd ever had until then had been lemon squash, I picked up the decanter and shook it vigorously. The heavens opened . . . But I suppose he was kind enough in his own strange way. He taught me the ways of country life: to ride, shoot, fish and so on, and I'm grateful for that. Even in his seventies he could outwalk me in my twenties—and I was then a Grenadier and in good physical shape.'

'When—or how—did you escape?'

'Well, when I was fourteen I was sent off to prep school, then to Harrow. After that I went to Sandhurst.'

'Why?'

'It was the only thing I seemed equipped for. I was good at games. I wasn't very bright in an academic way, a long way short of what's known as scholarship material. And although the Ansons have a great naval tradition, my father had been in the Brigade so I joined the army when I was seventeen and everybody in the family cheered. I was at Sandhurst for two years and then went into the Grenadiers for another four.'

Considering the well-known photographer, now so eminent a personality in swinging London, it is difficult to imagine him square-bashing on a parade ground or leading a platoon in the jungle, although his back is as flat as a bread-board and he moves almost always at the double, taking Shugborough's stairs, outdoors and indoors, four at a time.

'Did you enjoy the army?'

'Oddly enough, I did. At least, I enjoyed the real soldiering part—being overseas and all that. I certainly had no wish to kill anybody. I was less than keen for guard duty outside Buckingham Palace. But the army did teach me a kind of discipline, which has been useful, and the virtue of punctuality, rare, I gather, amongst photographers generally.'

'And after the Army?'

'I went to work for Dmitri Kasterine as dark room assistant and general dogsbody. I'd always been interested in photography and I wanted to learn the job properly. I owe a lot to Dmitri and later on I learned a lot from David Bailey.'

'And you also came back to Shugborough?'

'To the horrors of Shugborough as they then seemed to me. The death duties, which seemed astronomical; all the pictures gone; the roof showing signs of old age; the gardens rather a wilderness. A shambles all round.'

'You seem to have done a lot since.'

'Gradually with the help of my sister, who feels much the same way about Shugborough as I do myself. I suppose we both have a passion for the place, although it can never be ours the way other people's houses are their own. But we've come a long way, although there's still a long way to go. We've decorated our own quarters—with the help of David Mlinaric, of course. The National Trust does a marvellous job in the way they handle the visitors and all that. And so does the Staffordshire County Council, who took over the old stables and brewhouse. Under the directing genius of Mr. Geoffrey Wilding they've been turned into a magnificent local museum. Staffordshire ware, silver, uniforms, dresses, the flora and fauna of Cannock Chase and the rest.'

'Which part of the old Shugborough way of life do you most regret?'

Opposite (top to bottom) *The columns of the entrance front are made of slate ingeniously worked to give a fluted effect; the Temple of the Winds where the men used to gamble after dinner; the Doric Temple, built around 1758 by James 'Athenian' Stuart; the Chinese House, brought from the Far East by Admiral Anson*

'I regret nothing about Shugborough's old way of life. I much prefer my own, but, curiously enough, I desperately miss the pictures. I doubt whether there's another large house in Britain which has fewer worthwhile pictures. I miss those desperately.'

'Any in particular?'

'Not especially. Just the lot. Perhaps it's a feeling that grows in one. My first acquaintance with any of the pictures here was being ticked off for knocking a ping-pong ball against one of a pair of Zuccarellis. But I must have had an inkling of appreciation, for since we've learned that the one I bombarded was a fake and the one I left alone was the authentic one. Fortunately, both are still here, but in the main house.'

'What else went?'

'Furniture, silver, the lot. But, along with my trustees, I fought to keep the land. One can replace pictures, never land, or only rarely. And land, ultimately, always underpins a place like Shugborough. The great clean-out had its odd moments since. Last year I went to photograph the Onassis' yacht, the *Christina*, for American Vogue. The dining-room on board that floating palace is scarcely the normal idea of a yacht-style way of life. Taking a shot of the silver wine coasters on the centre table, I suddenly realised I was looking at my own crest. A curious twist.'

'What are you doing to replace things?'

'I'm *not* is the answer. Nowadays re-thinking is probably more rewarding than replacing. I'm beginning to buy modern pictures for one or two of the rooms. I think that the Albert Stadler, which I bought from the Kasmin Gallery is very successful against David's muddy-coloured walls. And I want to buy some pieces of furniture. But re-thinking's the main thing. That's why we asked David Mlinaric to decorate our part of the house. As you see, he's done a magnificent job.'

Agreement is easy, for the rooms are a visual delight, unlike any others in any other English Stately Home: dramatic, colourful, and practical.

'The house is unique, I think, for having decorations by John Fowler in the main house, and by the new generation, in the person of David, in our part of the house. Plus us, too, of course, for when we ran out of money for David, my sister, Liz, furnished the other rooms at an average cost of twenty-five pounds a room with the cheapest papers she could find in Stafford—and her own flair.'

'How do you arrange things with the National Trust?'

'Well, they have the main part of the house that the Ansons built and my sister and I have what was really the bedroom-nursery wing in my boyhood. I rent this wing from them on a recurring ninety-nine year lease. It seems to work quite well. It is less than a quarter of Shugborough and contains none of the State Rooms, but it serves us wonderfully well as a country house. I like entertaining here on a fairly large scale. We have enough bedrooms for that. We also have a splendid dining-room which David decorated in a very distinctively sombre way. We also have a fairly large formal sitting-room where everyone can sit around and talk after dinner or where we can listen to music and the rest. I was looking through the visitors' book the other day and found that we'd had something over three hundred guests here in two years—just about the same number that had been here during the previous twenty years.'

'Do you spend very much time here?'

'Not enough. Nowhere near enough. The trouble is I'm a professional photographer and that means going where the work is wanted and that means a great deal of travelling. I noticed in my passport last week that I'd been in thirty-six countries last year. It also means supplying the goods on time. I spend hours and hours in my dark room in London.'

Opposite, top *The staircase entrance to the flat*
Centre *Statue on the landing*
Bottom *The Main Hall, a square room made oval by the introduction of columns*

'You work for Vogue. Who else?'

'Well, for the Sunday Times, the Weekend Telegraph, Queen magazine and for advertising agencies.'

'What do you most enjoy?'

'Ultimately, I'd like to do photographic features on people like myself. Well, I mean people who are doing work they like doing. People whose work I like: artists, writers, musicians, architects, designers. The world's full of interesting people doing interesting things.'

'Do you find your social and professional worlds very different?'

'Very. Until I left the army I knew only the kind of people I'd grown up with. Then I moved into quite another world, a world I barely knew existed. I took to it immediately. Now I mix 'em.'

'And the result?'

'Works like a dream—with one major proviso. The people one mixes must all be good at what they're doing—and know they're pretty good. A successful racing motorist is immediately on terms with a successful landowner, and I daresay a dustman who's good at his job could hold his own with a duke who does a good job. I dunno. I've never tried that one. This social thing can be a big bore in England, but it never bothers me and it never seems to clutter up any of my relationships. All sorts come down here and it works. That's all I can say. I like my friends and acquaintances dropping in, whether they arrive by helicopter on the lawn or pay their half-crowns to see the house and then want to say hello to me.'

'Do you take much interest in the land here?'

'I try to be efficient in my own way of life and I like to know the farms are being efficiently run by the tenants here, for it's only out of the farm rents that Shugborough can be maintained and I can do the things that I think are needed.'

'What d'you particularly want to do? Make the place more beautiful generally or particularly?'

'Well, generally, of course, but I have a garden of my own here and I'd like to have a swimming pool there, well away from everyone. And I'd like to see some modern sculpture in the grounds. Things like that.'

'Do you mind the hordes descending on the house from Easter onwards?'

'A bit, but not desperately. After all, they help to keep me here. We need 'em is the short answer. And they must genuinely enjoy coming here, for we've no gimmicks and the numbers keep going up. We've nothing but the house to show 'em, plus the park and the museum—to my mind the finest country museum in England. We also have a wonderful collection of carriages and barouches in the stables, but they've always been here apart from a spectacularly beautiful coronation coach which Lord Shrewsbury's grandparents had and which he let us have when he left Ingestre.'

'Are you ever alone here?'

'Not often, but whenever I come here I like to spend at least twenty-four hours alone. Weekend parties are apt to start breaking-up early on Sunday afternoon. Then I can take a book up into the woods, or take a rod across to the river and unwind. I love it here. That's why I've been willing to give so much to it, for, make no mistake, this place—even my share of it—costs me packets a year out of my own pocket to run. I'd be a lot richer if it weren't for Shugborough, but I doubt whether I'd be any happier. Come and see the museum.'

And, with that, tall, erect, dressed in a royal blue high-waisted tweed suit with flared trousers and buckled shoes, Lord Lichfield leads the way out of the beautiful brown-fawn-subfusc toned sitting-room that Mlinaric evolved and strides along the fifty-yard corridor towards the side door that opens out from his private wing.

EBBERSTON HALL

EBBERSTON HALL, known until this century as Ebberston Lodge, was designed by Colin Campbell (died 1729) the friend of Lord Burlington. An elevation and plan of the house are reproduced in the third volume of Campbell's *Vitruvius Britannicus*. In his note to the engraving, the architect explains that the 'small rustick Edifice' was built for William Thompson in 1718 and goes on to describe the house as standing 'in a fine Park well planted, with a River, which forms a Cascade and Canal 1200 Feet long, and runs under the Loggio in the back Front.'

Colin Campbell, of whose early life in Scotland nothing is yet known, was at that time deputy to William Benson, then enjoying his short-lived tenure of the office of Surveyor-General, and in this connexion doubtless met Sir William Thompson, then Master of the Mint.

The design of Ebberston's unusual water gardens have been variously attributed to Stephen Switzer, author of *Universal System of waterworks Philosophical and Practical* (1734); Charles Bridgman, who had designed a water-garden for Thompson at Scampston in Yorkshire; and Benson himself.

Views of the house as it existed fairly soon after its completion are recorded in four paintings owned by Lord Hotham, whose family acquired the house half-a-century after its completion.

Comparing these paintings, now at Dalton Hall, with the engraving in *Vitruvius Britannicus*, certain amendments which were made to Campbell's original design in course of construction, or soon afterwards, are clearly recorded.

The wings were realigned to face south down the Vale of Pickering; a square cupola with an ogival roof was substituted for Campbell's more unusual and robust design of an octagonal base supporting a somewhat squat pyramidal terminal surmounted by a weather vane; and the specified ball finials to the parapet were superseded by urns.

The house was perhaps made 'prettier' by these innovations, but the authority and masculinity of Campbell's small 'Edifice', so well suited to its location, was undoubtedly diminished. Now, alas, the pavilions are no more, the cupola has gone, but enough remains to indicate the uniqueness of this small Palladian villa or 'casino' set so improbably in the Yorkshire dales.

Opposite *The North Front showing the pool, planned by Campbell as one of a series*

WEST AND MARGARET DE WEND-FENTON have lived at Ebberston Hall for almost twenty years. Despite its manifold inconveniences there is no doubt that they live in one of the most desirable homes in England.

Mr de Wend-Fenton's father bought the house with 80 acres, after seeing it knocked down—as part of a much larger estate—at an auction in the Talbot Hotel at Malton. He tackled the new owner and got his architectural toy-cum-gem with enough land to protect it from undue encroachment.

The present owner took over from his father in 1951. He had lived a fairly nomadic and adventurous life with stints in the French Foreign Legion in North Africa and as Queen's Messenger. His wife is a writer, currently engaged on the biography of her great, great grandmother, E.V.B. (the Hon. Mrs. Richard Boyle), a talented artist and writer known amongst specialist art historians for her illustrations for childrens' books.

The de Wend-Fentons have four children. The children and their friends inevitably adore the house, for it is exactly like some regal doll's house popped preposterously down in the West Riding of Yorkshire, between the dales and the sea.

'Many people, including some highly knowledgeable experts, have called this the most beautiful small great or great small house in England. Presumably, you'd agree.'

'I certainly think that it is a unique house in England in its style and beauty. Despite its constrictions and inconveniences as a family house we love the place. Italian villas aren't exactly designed for Yorkshire winters, as you can well imagine. The high rooms aren't easily heated, the back faces due north, the wind from the moors comes rushing down the valley and straight through this tiny house. Colin Campbell was plainly intent on effect rather than comfort. Even the first owner had the open loggia—which never sees the sun—walled-in after a few years. And when we came here the panelled walls were all painted over dark beige.'

'You soon altered that.'

'Not as soon as we would have liked. Shortly after we were married the Ministry of Works gave us a grant towards restoring the stonework of the façade and removing the dry rot from the panelling. The builders moved in almost immediately and there was nowhere to hide from them. They were with us for two dusty, draughty years, but we missed them after they'd gone. The house seemed so unnaturally quiet and tidy.'

'What were your own changes after the workmen had finished?'

'My husband gave the rooms the clear blues, greens and whites they deserved. His parents had filled the rooms with eighteenth-century furniture from the old family home in the West Riding. Then my husband again set to work to pick out the delicate carving with Woolworth gold paint. Even experts are deceived into thinking it's real gold leaf.'

'Have you changed the traditional arrangement of the rooms?'

'The only big change we made was to remove the dining-room to the loggia from the room next to the kitchen, where it had been for years. It's less convenient and I daresay labour-saving ultra-practical people would frown on the idea, but the lovely long room, with its view over the water garden and across the Vale of Pickering to the wolds is marvellous. And the mouldings on the wall, Bacchus and the dolphins, seemed to us to cry out for feasts to be celebrated there. We've never regretted the change for a minute, although it's a long run from the kitchen to the table. In summer, with the doors open, it's quite breathtaking.'

Above and Opposite *Mr and Mrs de Wend-Fenton and their four children outside the Entrance Front. The urns on the balustraded parapet replaced the original ball finials*

Fourposter bed with richly embroidered cover in one of the bedrooms
Opposite *The Drawing-Room is painted white, with the Corinthian capitals and other carving picked out in gold*

'Do you open so small a house to the public?'

'Having taken the grant, we had an obligation to open the house to the public. At first we did this with great enthusiasm and even opened a tea-room in the stables at the same time. It was a great success, although after wet Saturdays and Sundays when nobody came we were apt to live off our store of bacon and eggs all through the following week.'

'Do you still open to the public?'

'Oh, yes, but with four young children to look after, the tea-room has gone. We try to keep the house open at weekends, but sometimes measles, whooping-cough or some other juvenile disaster forces us to put the 'Closed' notice up.'

'Have the children grown up here?'

'Indeed, yes. Three of our babies were born here. That's why it's been necessary at times to explain to visitors why the bedrooms couldn't be seen. One of my babies was actually arriving when a group of sightseers knocked at the door. The nurse rushed from my room and I could hear her voice crying out "Sorry! Sorry! The house is closed. Mrs de Wend-Fenton is having a baby!" '

'Most of your visitors must find it pretty surprising to find a fairly large family living here in these modern times.'

'Some of them seem to—and make no bones about saying so. "When was this house last lived in normally?" the leader of one bus party demanded, gazing at me with a mildly disdainful look while the rest of her party surged past and fanned out to view the five small rooms. It was a day when my husband was away. From downstairs came the far-off yells of our three-month-old baby, left with propped-up bottle in her cradle. Sitting on the sofa of the white-panelled drawing-room, glowering at the visitors through shaggy locks of hair, was our two-year-old son. I had washed and dressed him in his best clothes a short hour before and sent him into the garden with instructions to keep tidy: but, like Tom Kitten, he had burst his buttons, tumbled down in the mud, and was in a disgraceful state. I, myself, was showing signs of the frantic morning I had spent, clearing away traces of our weekend guests, making beds, arranging flowers and shoving the usual junk, that always seems to accumulate around everyday living, into cupboards, drawers, under the beds, anywhere out of sight.'

'Didn't you hate them all?'

'No. In a way I could see their point of view. This beautiful tiny house, set like a little palace between the wooded slopes of the sleeping valley, seems to suggest carefree gracious living to match the surroundings. It's so easy to imagine a flurry of servants and strict, stiff-aproned Nannies in the background. But even if we could afford it, or wanted it, there wouldn't be any room for staff. Every inch of the house has, out of necessity, to be in constant use.'

'Even on less crowded and momentous days it must be rather a strain showing visitors around.'

'In a way, but we've got used to it. We found out quite early on that living in a small great house is paid for with a certain lack of privacy. In the great historic houses the owners can usually live in a wing or at least in private rooms set aside from the public eye. Here, the drawing-room, the dining-room and the bedrooms are pretty well the whole house. Anyone wanting to look at them must inevitably see our own lives going on at the same time. Life in this minute Palladian villa is very rarely as still and as perfect as the life in the Veneto that Palladio presumably had in mind—particularly with four children under twelve rushing around in the holidays, which is when the visitors come, of course.'

'What would you say were the major compensations for these drawbacks and problems?'

'Well, the summer brings compensations that outweigh any winter discomforts. The house, with its miniature rooms, seems to open out, light up and respond to sunlight and warmth. Then it's hard to imagine a more perfect place to live.'

'Who were your predecessors here?'

'Well, the most famous, or at least notorious, of them was undoubtedly Squire Osbaldeston in the nineteenth century, the self-styled 'Squire of All England'. He lived a hard-hunting, roistering life up here. Among his many sporting feats, done for a bet, was a ten-hour ride from York to London with a change of horses every four miles. Later on, when he got heavily into debt and was broke he'd take his furniture piece by piece up to the Grapes at Ebberston and barter it for drink. The pub's still owned by the same family, and they only sold the last of the Squire's furniture in nineteen-twenty or thereabouts. Osbaldeston used to take his favourite girl-friends up to the flat roof and trace the outlines of their tiny slippered feet on the stone parapet. The footmarks are there today, signed in the centre with nineteenth-century names like Harriet and Lucy. But I don't feel all that warm-hearted towards Osbaldeston. He said he found the place too small, added an ugly wing and was probably responsible for the

Above *View of the Entrance Hall from the Dining-Room which was originally an open loggia overlooking the water garden*
Opposite *The hall looking through to the Dining-Room.*

beginning of the deterioration of the formal and water gardens. With all his hunting, shooting and fishing activities he had no time for what must have been the most wonderful gardens, judging from a set of paintings of Ebberston which Lord Hotham owns.'

'Has anybody else of note lived here?'

'More recently a writer lived here. He emerges from the pages of his books as a kind of faint, fey shadow of St Francis of Assisi. He wrote of the place as 'a little fairy house surrounded by water and trickling streams'. He said he wanted to call it after Undine the water nymph, who got a soul by marrying a mortal. He also used the roof to sunbathe in a state of nature. Only the birds can see me, he said, but older members of the village can well remember, as children, getting a good view of him from the top of the hill.'

'What would be your ideal kind of existence here?'

'A quiet country life with open-house to one's own friends. I also have an impossible pipe dream, or is it a nightmare? One day I shall be sitting idly in the drawing-room after a leisurely luncheon on the terrace when an unexpected bus-load of sightseers arrives. Then I shall get up and meet them graciously, serene in the knowledge that there isn't an unmade bed, or a child turning out a chest of drawers, or my son's pet bantams invading the house from the back door, behind me.'

SEZINCOTE

JOHN COCKERELL, a Colonel in the East India Company establishment in India, acquired Sezincote from the Earl of Guilford in 1795, but died three years later. He left his property equally to his two younger brothers: Sir Charles Cockerell, who had also served profitably in India, and Samuel Pepys Cockerell, then in his forties and a well-established architect, with Admiralty House amongst other well-known buildings to his credit.

Sir Charles and his younger brother seem not to have set about building the present house at Sezincote until about 1805, by which time they had decided to build on the site of an earlier house. Cockerell had already had some experience in designing in a mildly oriental form at nearby Daylesford which he had built for Warren Hastings between 1790 and 1796. In that house he had been responsible for introducing highly ornamental furnishings, in the so-called Hindoo taste, into what was basically a neo-classical shell. He was to repeat the exercise at Sezincote, although from its inception, the latter was intended to be a far more exotic house in every way.

At a very early stage in their deliberations, the two brothers seem to have consulted Thomas Daniell, who, with his nephew, William, was to publish the notable *Oriental Scenery* a record of Indian buildings and landscapes in 1808. Daniell seems to have discussed the project at length with the brothers who must have worked together with rare fraternal understanding and sympathy. As an essay in combining the neo-classical canons of Europe with the architectural exoticism of the Orient Sezincote thus had sound beginnings.

The dominant feature of the exterior is, of course, the turquoise-coloured, copper-covered, onion-shaped dome set on a podium surmounting the low-pitched roof of the house. The podium and the rooftop carry parapets of oriental derivation. Sezincote is also remarkable for its wide soffits or *chujja* which overhang a highly decorative cornice-cum-frieze. In bright sunlight these pronounced soffits give emphatic shadows to the walls. Great care was taken by the architect to ensure authentic decorative detail in the carving of the brackets, which supported the *chujja*; also in the carving of parapets, window recesses and walls. This careful supervision also extends to the Moghul-inspired designs of the cast-metal verandahs of the house and to the exterior fences. The low-pitched roof with its parapet, chimneys and *chattris* (cowled finials) at the corners emphasizes the eastern nature of the house.

Because the house is basically of two storeys, Cockerell's plan has a long frontage to accommodate the reception rooms, owners' bedrooms and staff requirements. Sir Charles' own bedroom, curiously enough, was at the extreme end of the north wing pavilion, which is counter-balanced to the south by the magnificent curving greenhouse also terminating in a pavilion.

This strange oriental fantasy set so unexpectedly in the Cotswolds now seems, paradoxically enough, completely at home. The English landscape with its immense capacity for absorbing the most diverse elements has here accomplished one of its most satisfying syntheses.

Opposite *Views of Sezincote and the Orangery from various points in the park*

SEZINCOTE lies high in the Cotswolds between Stow-on-the-Wold and Moreton-in-the-Marsh, as improbable a building to find in the English countryside as that regal Moghul folly on the lawns of Brighton.

The house is hidden from all but invited eyes, at the end of a mile-long drive. No architectural exuberance at the lodge gives any indication of the fantasy within.

The visitor passes a forgotten cottage, part Gothic, part Indian, half-way along the drive, but the bizarre serenity of Sezincote still comes as something of a visual shock at journey's end: an oriental fantasy, set athwart a gravelled forecourt on a modest plateau overlooking a magnificent Cotswold landscape, timbered ridge upon ridge to the distant hills. With its copper-covered onion dome; delicate corner finials (or *chattris*); widely overhanging soffit (or *chuija*); octagonal pavilion terminating an intricately glazed Orangery, and windows as fanciful as any to be seen in the East, the house is clearly a mansion out of a fairy-tale.

Sir Charles Cockerell, whose family had long had connexions with the East India Company and who had made a sizable fortune for himself in India, was the sponsor of this oriental fantasy. Sir Charles was clearly a man of taste, individuality, and resolution. More to the point, he was unusually fortunate in his near relations. He had been left part of the manor of Sezincote by his elder brother, and his younger brother, Samuel Pepys, sold him his share and also became his architect.

Samuel Pepys Cockerell was about fifty, an established and successful architect, when he was offered this fraternal commission in about 1805. He had already experimented in a mild kind of way with various forms of Anglo-Indian decoration at nearby Daylesford, which he had designed for Warren Hastings and supervised in its building between 1790 and 1796.

Sir Charles must have seen Daylesford and liked what he saw, and it says much for the relationship that must have existed between the two brothers, for Sir Charles, apparently, requested no alternative designs from any other architect, although Thomas Daniell was responsible for all the detail in the stonework of the exterior and Repton was later consulted concerning the landscaping of the gardens.

Certainly the house when built must have pleased Sir Charles, for it is uncommonly successful both as a curious, even spectacular, self-indulgence in the oriental manner, but also as a practical and comfortable house in which to live. Although the house was originally a good deal larger than it is today, it was eminently suitable for its period, being basically a two-storey structure and offering even the plurality of domestic staff of those days no undue mileage of corridors and stairways.

But when Mr and Mrs Cyril Kleinwort first saw Sezincote on a summer's day in the middle of the war, the mansion seemed to offer dauntingly few of these practicalities. They had seen the house advertised in *Country Life* and journeyed to Stow almost as an excuse for an excursion during one of Mr Kleinwort's rare days of leave from the Admiralty, where he was then serving as an officer in the Volunteer Reserve.

Sezincote was owned by a Mrs Dugdale who was living in the large house almost in siege conditions. The house was cold and bleak and showed only too clearly the manifold signs of wartime wear and tear. Above all it was obviously far too large a house for any kind of reasonable comfort in what promised to be the emphatically changed conditions of post-war Britain. But Betty Kleinwort, whilst still remembering these things, recalls no undue moments of trepidation.

Opposite, above *The Saloon with its great bow window and pelmet treatment following the style established by Cockerell*
Below *The Drawing-Room*

Above, left and Opposite *Two views of the curving staircase. On the first floor are two eighteenth-century Aubusson tapestries*
Above right *Chandelier at the top of the staircase*

'What persuaded you to take the house, then?'

'Heaven knows. Its sheer strangeness perhaps. The marvellous surroundings which even the war couldn't diminish. Also, I suppose, my husband's conviction that we might be able to reduce the house to a manageable size. And he usually turns out to be right.'

'Did you lose your nerve at all?'

'No. Surprisingly, perhaps, I never felt worried about it.'

'When did you move in?'

'In 'forty-six. My husband had left the Navy by then, of course, and gone back into the City.'

'How did you get the house straight?'

'Sheer perseverance, persistence, energy. And we were very lucky in that our staff from our old house came with us. But it was uphill work, complicated by the fact that in those first post-war years any building work could only be carried out by government licence with a limit of something like a hundred pounds. Anyway, the allowances were always far short of what we needed. Luxuries were certainly out, although, I suppose, licences did keep one from overspending and all that. But it was infinitely galling sometimes to be unable to do essential things, even to the very fabric of the house, in case one was breaking the law. But gradually, as things got easier and regulations were relaxed, we were able to press on.'

'Presumably you did reduce the size of the house substantially?'

'Quite considerably, but happily, what we took down didn't in any way impair Cockerell's general design. Even though we incorporated Sir Charles' octagonal bedroom (which was way out on the north wing) into

Opposite *A view of the intricately glazed Orangery*
Above *Looking from the Orangery door to the house*
Right *The magnificent bed, constructed from ornamental spears, from Sir Charles Cockerell's own bedroom in the octagonal pavilion, now converted into cottages*

staff cottages, the architectural pundits seem to agree that we behaved very sympathetically, which is always a comfort to anybody living in an historic house.'

'Did the oriental background present any problems as far as decorating was concerned?'

'Here and there, inevitably, although the interior of the house is in fact neo-classical, so we didn't have to play up to any oriental theme. Round-headed windows aren't the easiest windows in the world to curtain, and to start with we had to adapt our existing curtains. Later, I met John Fowler and was able to call on his expertise for our two principal rooms. He's been a great friend and ally in the whole enterprise, although he's such a perfectionist, decoratively and historically, so to speak, that he's sometimes a bit difficult for ordinary mortals to live up to. But we've stayed friends, so I suppose that says everything.'

'You seem to have been far luckier than many owners of historic houses. You've kept the place to yourselves and not had to open the place up and all that.'

'Well, Sezincote's not what you'd call a Stately Home, is it? I always think of it as a large small house or a small large house, depending on the kind of day it is, and how things are going. Anyway it's quite manageable, which is the main thing these days.'

'Large small house or small large house, one or two of the rooms wouldn't be out of place in a palace, wouldn't you say?'

'Well, the Saloon really is a gorgeous room, with those three magnificent windows. Fortunately, we've been able to keep it much the same as I

gather it always was. Those elaborate draped pelmets are illustrated in *Ackermann's Repository*. They were rose-pink then, but our curtains are in yellow silk.'

'The stately bedroom also seems to have something of a Xanadu touch about it.'

'Well, we made the bed from a set of ornamental spears which Sir Charles seems to have used as supports for his own tent-shaped bedroom which, as I said, used to be over in the octagonal pavilion in the north wing. Stanley Peters decorated this room and he asked Geoffrey Ghin to paint the *trompe-l'œil* screen for it, the one showing a young Regency sprig looking out towards the house from the greenhouse. It's very successful, I think, but our own bedrooms are on a somewhat less flamboyant scale, I'm happy to say.'

'The Hall at Sezincote always seems an architectural *tour de force*. Magnificent, but not one of those great soaring jobs going off to the clouds.'

'That's one of the nicest things about Sezincote. Nothing is too overpowering. And the staircase, with its splendid curves, is beautifully designed.'

'But you'll admit the gardens here outdo those of most Stately Homes.'

'Well, they've certainly become rather a passion. One can't own gardens

Above *The house seen beyond an ornamental pavilion in the garden*
Opposite, above *The oriental shrine with the figure of Souriya, goddess of Pity, probably attributable to Thomas Daniell*
Below *One of the statues of sacred Brahmin cows on the oriental bridge*

as exotic, beautiful and historic as these without wanting to keep them up and to try to improve them. Fortunately, our gardener here loves the place almost as much as we do.'

Any perambulation of the garden at Sezincote is more like a walk through some legendary garden in the foothills of the Himalayas than a walk through a Cotswold pleasance. The landscaping probably owes much of its exotic splendour to Thomas Daniell, that artist renowned for his great work, *Oriental Scenery*, based on drawings and water-colours made in India during a decade or more before Sezincote was built. Daniell seems to have been on friendly terms with the Cockerell brothers and undoubtedly showed them some of his unpublished drawings. To him, therefore, is probably due the credit for the conception of the Temple Pool, with its oriental shrine and its figure of Souriya, the goddess of Pity. Lower, an oriental bridge spans another pool. The garden is a perfect example of the English natural garden linked with evocations of the East, part factual, part fanciful. With its encompassing woodlands of rare evergreens and other exotic trees it is one of the most spectacular and enchanting in Europe. The basic design still owes a great deal to Repton and is now tenderly and knowledgeably maintained by the Kleinworts.

Few houses and gardens in the world compose so magically into this perfect synthesis of stone, plants and water as Sezincote in Gloucestershire.

THE ROYAL PAVILION

THE ORIGINAL Royal Pavilion at Brighton, designed by Henry Holland, was built at a speed that would daunt most twentieth-century builders. It was started in April 1787 and the Prince Regent moved in early in July. He moved into an elegant classical villa in the Palladian manner, faced with Holland's favourite 'mathematical' tiles and with those canopied, balconied bow windows which were to be charming features of the houses that were later to be built in Brighton's Kemp Town. The building and decoration cost £13,450.

This comparatively modest establishment, however, soon proved too small for the Prince's expansive outlook after his reconciliation with Mrs Fitzherbert following the breakdown of his marriage to Princess Caroline of Brunswick. Holland's assistant, P F Robinson, added two oval-shaped wings, but these and other contemplated additions were overtaken by the Prince's sudden and, by then, somewhat belated passion for Chinese decorative influences, thanks to a gift of several pieces of Chinese wallpapers. The Prince's own rooms were soon given over to *chinoiserie*, and chinese columns in the Music Room were painted with dragons. Chinese furniture and porcelain was added, some from the Prince's London establishment at Carlton House, other pieces by purchase. So enchanted was the Prince by this vision of Cathay that during the next decade he commissioned various projects for giving the Pavilion a Chinese exterior, but his astronomical debts and unpopularity delayed any start on the venture.

Thanks to a rising interest in Indian architecture, fostered partly by the aquatints of Thomas and William Daniell, and by the building of Sezincote, the Prince moved away from Chinese to Moghul preoccupations, a transition seen first in the domed stables near the Pavilion. This move was aided by the suggested plans for the Pavilion gardens outlined by Humphrey Repton, fresh from advice at Sezincote. Once again, however, lack of funds circumscribed the Prince's architectural ambitions.

The Pavilion that we see today is basically the work of John Nash (a friend of Repton's, whose sons worked for him) who was also a member of the Prince's set and had also acted as his architect for the conversion of Cumberland Lodge in Windsor Park into the Royal Lodge. From 1815 onwards he began the conversion of the Pavilion into an oriental fantasy. The project gave Nash full scope for his brilliant and inventive genius, resulting in that triumph of 'picturesque Orientalism' which has astonished and enchanted successive generations of visitors to Brighton. Contrary to many accusations of jerry-building levelled against Nash for his work in Regent's Park, the structural work of the Pavilion is of high quality.

The main part of the Pavilion was completed in 1818, although a new suite of apartments for the Prince was started the following year. The decorating of the interior continued for another four years.

The total cost of the Royal Pavilion was around half-a-million pounds, a fantastic sum for those days. The expenditure aroused much political and journalistic criticism. Today, visitors to Britain can look more tolerantly upon this regal extravagance.

Opposite, above (*left to right*) *The King's Library and Ante Room; the fireplace in the long corridor; part of the North Drawing-Room, formerly the Music Room Gallery*
Below *Examples of the gilt dolphin furniture, made in memory of Lord Nelson, in the South Drawing-Room*

Opposite, above *Bedroom furnished with Princess Charlotte's furniture*
Below *A bedroom furnished in early-Victorian style with half-tester brass bedstead*
Right *The King's bedroom. The bed was originally a simple French example, now replaced by a nineteenth-century Chinoiserie design. The rest of the furniture is mainly of black and gold lacquer*

CLIFFORD MUSGRAVE, librarian-turned-museum-director-turned-art-historian, looks the part: a slim, donnish man, above middle height, with an amused smile never far away and a liveliness of mind and vigour of stride belying, by a decade or more, his sixty-odd years. He is less-than-donnish in his views: articulate, vigorous, sharply lively. And very much of our own time.

To him, more than to any other man, group, society or committee, Brighton owes the continued existence of the Royal Pavilion as a vivid evocation of a wayward but stylish monarch's unique palace-cum-retreat.

Mr Musgrave went to Brighton in 1939 as Chief Librarian and Curator to the Brighton Corporation. He had served his apprenticeship in the Public Reference Library at Croydon, and later was in charge of libraries and museums in several smaller towns. He came to Brighton from Birkenhead where the Williamson Art Gallery is one of the finest buildings of its kind and possesses one of the best provincial collections in the country, but is still one of the least known.

Almost as soon as he had taken up his new duties the Second World War began, and in no time at all he found the Royal Pavilion on his hands as a responsibility supernumerary to books and museum specimens.

Pre-war, the Royal Pavilion was not the profitable showpiece it is today. In the year before the war something under £300 was taken in entrance fees from the public, representing rather fewer than 5,000 visitors. Nowadays, almost half-a-million annual visitors are willing to pay £50,000 for the pleasure of their journey into one of the most spectacular regal follies in Europe.

Mr Musgrave retired in August last year, handing over to John Morley, previously in charge of the Bradford Art Gallery. Now, after twenty years' residence in the Pavilion, he lives in a small house along the coast near Rottingdean. Here he prepares his lectures and writes his scholarly books on architecture and furniture, although the book he has recently completed is a monumental study of life in Brighton through the centuries.

'How did you react to being given charge of such an extraordinary building as the Pavilion? It could have been a startling experience—almost traumatic!'

'It was certainly an exciting and unexpected happening, but in a sense I had been preparing for it for years. I had always been interested in the classical world—everything stems from that—and during the 'twenties and 'thirties I became more and more fascinated by the eighteenth century, especially architecture and the cult of the Picturesque—landscape gardening, *chinoiserie*, follies and the off-beat crazes of the world, but I had nothing to exercise my interest upon. It was all in a vacuum. When I came to Brighton the late Professor Sir Charles Reilly was on my committee and knew about these interests of mine. I believe he had something to do with my being given charge of the Pavilion.'

To the question: 'Did you enjoy your Royal Pavilion stint?' he replies unequivocally: 'It was a marvellous experience in furniture, architecture and men. During the war the Pavilion was merely under my charge for care and maintenance. The place had a vastly different life then from what it enjoys today. We had any number of public meetings and military courses going on there, but little interest in the architecture, and no furniture to speak of.'

'What were your first ventures in furnishing the building?'

'One had naturally cherished the seemingly hopeless idea of having the

Opposite, above *The room restored as an early nineteenth-century drawing-room, furnished chiefly with satinwood pieces, of Sheraton design, originally belonging to Mrs Fitzherbert*
Below *The Great Kitchen remains almost exactly the same as shown in Ackerman's aquatint with the original revolving spits, bronze smoke canopies and lanterns*

original furniture returned from Buckingham Palace, but the first success in this direction was through the inspiration of Lady Birley who, with a private committee in conjunction with the Corporation, organized the first Regency Exhibition of 1946 for charity, with furniture lent by King George VI and Queen Elizabeth, now the Queen Mother. Two similar exhibitions were held under the same auspices in 1948 and 1951, but after that the private committee was dissolved and the Regency Exhibitions became annual events run entirely under the Corporation.

'From the beginning the exhibitions were a tremendous success. The flamboyant splendour and quality of the Regency style had an especial appeal after wartime austerity and utility furniture, and the interest of the public was also aroused by the visits of Queen Mary, Queen Elizabeth the Queen Mother and other members of the Royal Family to the exhibitions.'

'How did you stock the early exhibitions? Were you always able to borrow the original furniture?'

'No. The furniture from Buckingham Palace had to be returned in the early days, but we borrowed largely from private collectors and from the antique dealers, who were remarkably co-operative and who found that our shows had a remarkable effect in developing an interest in the Regency period. We also borrowed splendid collections of silver from the V & A, the National Trust, the City of London, and the Royal Artillery.'

'What happened when you did begin to air your ideas?'

'Well, in the earliest days of the restoration, some members of the Corporation and public didn't quite see eye-to-eye with me, but the Pavilion Committee was always tolerant and supported me. As my odd notions began to prove themselves—and began to prove profitable to Brighton's coffers—things inevitably began to get easier.'

'First of all, from 1950 onwards the Corporation spent over eighty thousand pounds in restoring the fabric of the building—they certainly deserve a national vote of thanks for that.'

'How did you start getting the interior decorations restored, the way they are today?'

'Fortunately the hour always seemed to produce the man. I was lucky in gathering round me a remarkable team of assistants, including Roy Bradley, a gifted interior decorator. We also acquired the services of some highly talented craftsmen—cabinet-makers, metal-workers, painters and gilders. Few of them had done work of the quality—and, let's face it, oddity—that was needed at the Pavilion, but they soon learned.'

'Who were your first backers?'

'My very first was my wife, Margaret. Most of the best ideas for colour schemes and decoration came from her. She'd studied under Tonks at the Slade, and had also attended Professor Richardson's lectures at the Bartlett School. So she'd done her homework. Not only that, but she also saved me from the occasional disaster in municipal life by her tact and foresight. They're not my major talents.'

'How did you proceed—or get your own way, so to speak?'

'Gradually was the word. Gradually we got more and more ambitious—perhaps audacious would be more accurate—in what we were trying to do and we soon began to discover that people liked what they saw.'

'What about your Committee? Did they back you all the way?'

'Well, there again I was very lucky. Committees in the immediate post-war years were far more flexible in their reactions and attitudes than they're apt to be today. Brighton is growing all the time, of course, and getting more and more managerial in its methods. I suppose things have to be that way, but I'm glad my time came when it did. My outfit was

Opposite *The Indian domes, minarets, pinnacles and pagoda roofs added to the Royal Pavilion by John Nash between 1815 and 1822*

sympathetic from the beginning. When they saw that it was becoming a significant feature of the Brighton scene they really gave me a free hand.'

'How did the original furniture come to be returned from Buckingham Palace permanently?'

'We had the good fortune to be visited in 1951 by the Queen, who was then Princess Elizabeth. It was out of the exhibition season, and walking through the empty rooms she remarked upon the absence of the original furniture, which she was familiar with at Buckingham Palace.'

'Eventually, and thanks no doubt too, in part, to the good offices of the Queen's advisors, Oliver Millar and Francis Watson, over a hundred of the original pieces from the Royal Pavilion came back to their original home on permanent loan. That was in 'fifty-five.'

'Quite a scoop!'

'It was, indeed. I've rarely been more excited in my life.'

'Was it difficult to find the right places for them?'

'Not very. From old prints and records we knew where many of the pieces had originally stood. But the gift did cause us to look afresh at the Pavilion. For instance, putting the cabinets which had been made for the Corridor back in place more or less demanded a repainting of the wall decorations.'

'A tricky job?'

'Very. A complicated matter indeed. A lot of research and a great deal of work. The decoration was finally painted in oil on cartridge paper spread upon linen stretched over the timber-boarded walls. But we're pretty certain, judging from existing fragments, that we now have an authentic copy of the original scheme.'

'What about the rest of the treasure-trove?'

'Well, we've had two other great strokes of good fortune. First, we were enabled to have on loan here a selection of the silver-gilt pieces from the Marquess of Ormonde's Collection which had been on loan to the V & A. And we were equally fortunate in having on loan some of the magnificent Londonderry Collection bought by Lord Stewart, later the Marquess of Londonderry, before his appointment as ambassador to Vienna during the Napoleonic wars. The pieces we had from both collections have made an enormous difference to the displays we like to put on in the Banqueting Hall. After all, it's not much fun having that vast place without the spectacular kind of display that got laid on for State Banquets in George the Fourth's time.'

'Which do you think is the most authentic room in the Pavilion?'

'In a way all the rooms are now pretty authentic—in feeling at least. To most visitors, of course, the Great Kitchen always seems the *pièce de resistance*, so to speak. The Kitchen visitors see today matches almost knife for knife the scene shown in Ackerman's aquatint of a banquet in preparation.'

'Do you still buy any furniture?'

'As the Pavilion became more popular and successful financially, and thus more of an asset to Brighton, I was given an annual allotment of two thousand pounds for furniture. Even less than twenty years ago one could do a lot with that. By judicious buying and expert help we were able to do quite a lot.'

'Where particularly?'

'Not, as you might think, in the more spectacular State Rooms but in two of my favourite smaller rooms on the first floor. One of the rooms we restored and furnished as an early-nineteenth-century drawing-room, chiefly with satinwood pieces of Sheraton design which had originally belonged to the king's longtime favourite, Mrs Fitzherbert. The story is curious. They were part of that lady's furniture which was sold when she finally parted from the Prince Regent in eighteen-eleven. Her creditors sold up her furniture. This suite was bought by a Colonel Greenwood. His family had it for eighty years. Then it passed to other owners, re-appearing in the market as two groups in nineteen-fifty-two. Sir Albert Richardson bought one group and we bought the other group two years later.'

'Well, it all looks beautifully at home. Which is the other room?'

'That's another odd story. This room is the bedroom probably used by Princess Charlotte during her visit in eighteen-sixteen and -seventeen. A pair of washstands of Chinese design was found in a Worthing dealer's. After the brown paint was removed the branded GR Pavilion cypher was discovered. A set of landscapes painted in China and backed by Pavilion dragon-pattern wallpaper was discovered by Derek Rogers, this time in a Brighton shop. Little wonder I've a soft spot for these two rooms so adventurously put together again.'

'How do you see the Pavilion yourself?'

'Well, I don't think I can do better than paraphrase a passage from the book I wrote on the Pavilion. For me, it expresses the delightful paradoxes of the Regency age to perfection. Here we see the fusion of the classical with the romantic, the intellectual and the poetic, the picturesque and the functional. And if one building can manage all that—as I think the Royal Pavilion does—I think it deserves a visit, don't you?'

Below *The dome of the Music Room with its waterlily chandeliers and immense wall-paintings of Chinese landscapes in scarlet, gold and yellow lacquer*